BULGING BRAINS

Nick Arnold and Tony De Saulles

SCHOLASTIC

www.scholastic.co.uk

Scholastic Children's Books,
Euston House, 24 Eversholt Street,
London NW1 1DB, UK

A division of Scholastic Ltd
London ~ New York ~ Toronto ~ Sydney ~ Auckland
Mexico City ~ New Delhi ~ Hong Kong

First published in the UK by Scholastic Ltd, 1999
This revised and updated edition published by Scholastic Ltd, 2014

ISBN 978 1407 14264 7

Printed and bound by CPI Group (UK) Ltd, Croydon, CR0 4YY

2 4 6 8 10 9 7 5 3 1

CONTENTS

Nick Arnold has been writing stories and books since he was a youngster, but never dreamt he'd find fame writing about body bits. His research involved volunteering for brain surgery and checking his reflexes with a giant hammer and he enjoyed every minute of it.

When he's not delving into Horrible Science, he spends his spare time eating pizza, riding his bike and thinking up corny jokes (though not all at the same time).

www.nickarnold-website.com

Tony De Saulles picked up his crayons when he was still in nappies and has been doodling ever since. He takes Horrible Science very seriously and even agreed to sketch Nick's brain operation. Fortunately, it didn't make him feel too poorly.

When he's not out with his sketchpad, Tony likes to write poetry and play squash, though he hasn't written any poetry about squash yet.

www.tonydesaulles.co.uk

INTRODUCTION

To hear some scientists talk you'd think they knew everything about science...

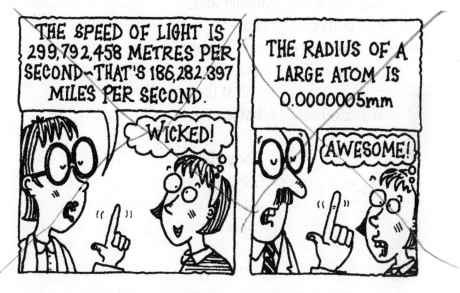

But don't be fooled – scientists *don't* know everything. After all, if they did there would be no need for any new experiments. Scientists could sit around all day with their feet up. But, in fact, there are lots of mysteries left to solve. Lots of things we don't know or don't understand.

For example, there's one object that's so mysterious it makes even a brainy scientist scratch their head. It's wet and squishy and looks revolting – and oddly enough, it's found between their ears. What is it? No, it's not their disgusting, snotty nose. It's the bit *inside* their head – their bulging brain. Scientists aren't too sure how it works…

But if scientists are puzzled by their own little grey cells what chance do the rest of us have? No wonder learning about your brain can make your head ache.

Well, if science scrambles your brains, help is at hand. This book is bulging with brain facts. For example, bet you never knew that in 1998 US scientists found the part of the brain that makes you laugh. They gave an electric shock to this area of a girl's brain and she started giggling uncontrollably.

And that's not all. Did you know that in one brain experiment children were forced to sniff their little brothers' stinky old T-shirts? (See page 69 for all the smelly details.) Now that really is cruelty!

So by the time you've finished reading this book your knowledge will be so vast you could easily become the brains of your class. And who knows?

Your teacher might even mistake you for a scientific mega-genius. But to enjoy the full benefits you've got to ask your brain to help you read this book.

Your eyeballs scan the letters, your brain makes sense of the words, and your memory reminds you what they mean. But hold on – looks like you've already started … oh well, don't let me stop you. Oh, and once you've read page 9 you'll need to ask your brain to send a message down thousands of nerves to tell your finger muscles to gently lift the next page.

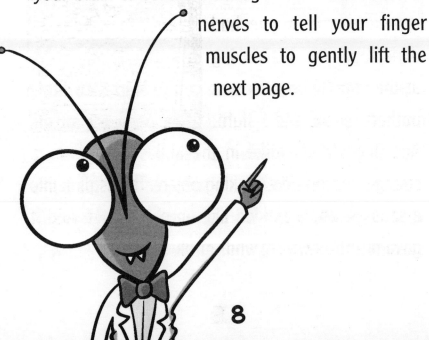

BULGING BRAIN BASICS

Dr Funkenstain felt a rush of excitement as she gazed into the glass tank. For five years she had been planning this experiment. Now she had done it and she was looking at the result. The tank was bathed in an eerie light. And floating ghostlike in the tank's centre was a strange and horrible looking object. It was pink like a sausage and wrinkled like an old walnut. And it gave out the faintest whiff of blue cheese.

Could it be an unknown creature from the depths of the ocean? Or perhaps an alien from another world? Dr Funkenstain knew better. She was gazing at a real human brain. A very special human brain because…

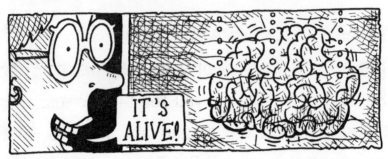

Dr Funkenstain whispered excitedly. Peering closer she could see the tiny wormlike blood vessels criss-crossing the brain's surface. Dr Funkenstain had done it. She was the first scientist in history to keep a brain alive outside the body.

DON'T PANIC! It's only a story. Scientists can't keep human brains in tanks – yet. But this technique might be possible in the future. Perhaps you'd like to become the first brain surgeon to keep a brain in a tank? If so beware: it's a bad idea to rush into brain surgery without getting to know a bit about your subject. Important facts like…

WHAT'S YOUR BRAIN FOR?

The brain is the part of your body that tells you what's going on around you. You can use your brain to order your body around and even to order everybody else around. But there's much more to your brain. Much, much more.

Inside your brain are your precious memories, your dreams, your hopes for the future and the knowledge of everything you love and care about. In your brain you can sense lovely smells and tastes and colours. Your brain helps you feel great and happy about life and that's the good side. But your brain also creates horrible fears and worries that can make you miserable.

Your brain makes the thoughts and feelings that make your personality. Your brain turns your body from a living object into *you* the person. Without a brain you'd be as dead as a dodo's tombstone, so it's good to know that you've got your very own bulging brain right now between your ears ... hopefully.

INSIDE THE BULGING BRAIN

Still want to be a brain surgeon? Excellent. Now you've found out a bit about what the bulging brain does, you're ready to check out how it works...

BET YOU NEVER KNEW!

Your brain weighs less than 1.3 kg – that's a little less than the weight of a large bag of sugar or the weight of all the germs swarming in your guts. In fact, the brain is only one-fiftieth the weight of a grown-up man and it's far lighter than your guts, your blood, your skin or your bones.

HAVE YOU GOT A BULGING BRAIN?

So just how clever is your brain? Well, if you're going to be a brain surgeon you'll need to know all the answers to this brain-teasing quiz:

1 What happens if half your brain is damaged?

a) It doesn't half hurt, ha-ha. No, seriously, you can't remember anything.

SORRY, WHAT WAS THE QUESTION AGAIN?

b) You die. No one could survive such a terrible injury.

c) You can live normally although you have to re-learn vital skills such as talking.

2 What happens if someone cuts your brain in two?

a) Your brain becomes twice as clever.

b) Your brain functions normally but

you may find yourself doing your science homework twice.

c) Each side of your brain behaves like a separate person.

3 Imagine you were born without 97 per cent of your cortex (cor-tex) — that's the wrinkly part of your brain at the top where you do your thinking. You're left with a tiny slice of brain in this area. What would happen to you?
a) You'd be left with the brains of a half-witted stick insect.
b) You'd be as brainy as anyone else … but only for five minutes a day. The rest of the time you'd blunder around like a zombie in a horror movie.
c) Your brain would work normally and you could be as brainy as your science teacher. (Yes, teachers are said to be intelligent.)

4 What would you feel if someone stuck a finger into your brain and waggled it about?
a) Unbearable agony — the worst pain in the world.
b) You'd feel hot and cold shivers all over your body.
c) Nothing because the brain cannot feel touch.

5 How much energy does your brain use in a science test?
a) Such a small amount that it can't be measured (especially if you don't know the answers).
b) Enough to light up the classroom. No wonder the test makes you light-headed, ha-ha.
c) Just enough to power a dim light bulb.

6 Why do you feel tired after the test?

a) All that mental effort strains the brain.

b) During the test your brain drew extra energy in the form of sugar in your blood. After the test your body feels tired because it lacks this vital blood sugar.

c) You were so tense your muscles bunched up and used up energy. And your muscles feel tired — not your brain.

7 How much of your brain is water?

a) About 5 per cent

b) 32 per cent

c) About 80 per cent

All the answers are **c)**, so you can check them without taxing your brain too much. And here are a few more details to get you thinking.

1 A bump on the head can injure the brain (see page 171 for the grisly details). Yet the brain can survive dreadful injuries. If one half of the brain is injured, the half that's left learns how to do the work of the damaged half.

2 This operation was performed in the 1960s on patients suffering from violent fits. The operation stopped the fits from spreading through the brain. But afterwards the two sides of the brain acted like separate people. One woman tried to put on a different shirt with each hand. She ended up wearing two shirts.

3 People can live a normal life with very little cortex. This can be the result of a condition called hydrocephalus (hi-dro-cef-al-us). This results in too much fluid sloshing around the skull, so there's less room for the brain.

4 Your nerves take signals from elsewhere in your body to your brain. This means you actually experience pain, touch, taste, smell, sound and vision in your brain. But oddly enough, there are no touch sensors on the brain itself. (You'll find the low-down on senses from page 58.)

5 Yes, in light bulb terms we're all rather dim. Scientist Louis Sokoloff of the US National Institute of Mental Health has found the brain uses the same amount of energy gazing dreamily at a sunset as it does in a tough science test. So what would you rather do?

6 If the questions were really easy, and you managed to relax in the science test, you wouldn't feel so whacked.

7 That's why when you become a brain surgeon and get to touch a brain it'll feel like squidgy blancmange or a soft-boiled egg. The brain needs water for vital chemical reactions such as sending nerve signals. Without water, a brain begins to overheat and starts to see things that aren't there. Ultimately it will die.

BULGING BRAIN SECRETS

Psst – wanna know a brain secret? There's more to your brain than water. For example, your brain's made up of millions of cells and each one is so small you need a microscope to see it. (No, these aren't cells that people get locked up in.) Read on, your brain might learn something…

BULGING BRAIN CELLS

1 Your brain is bulging with 100,000,000,000 – that's 100 *billion* – nerve cells or neurons. These are special cells used for sending signals inside the brain. If you don't believe it, try counting them yourself.

2 Each cell is a living blob and some are so tiny that you can fit 25 on to this full stop. (You'll need a steady hand for this.)

3 If you laid the cells from just one brain in a line they would stretch 1,000 km – a quarter of the way across the USA.

4 Unborn babies grow about 2,000 new neurons every second, but by the time you reach 25, 12,000 of your neurons are dying off every day (that's 4.4 million a year). DON'T PANIC – parts of your brain grow new neurons. For example, new neurons grow in the part of your brain that deals with smelling – and that really is something to get sniffy about.

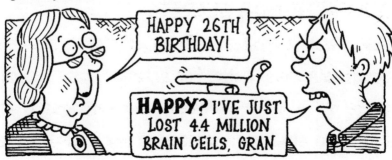

And anyway you won't run out of neurons. You can live a long life and still have 98 per cent of them left.

5 Your brain cells are hungry for blood. No, they're not vampires – they need the sugars and oxygen that blood carries. Your brain sucks in 750 ml of the red stuff every minute. And if your brain doesn't get enough blood, it goes on strike and switches itself off. You might call this fainting.

OK, so now you know the brain basics – and that's more than the first brain boffins. When they started to study the brain they knew nothing. Everything was a massive maddening mystery. Check out the next page and prepare to be baffled, bewildered, bemused and *brain-boggled.*

BULGING BRAIN BOFFINS

The first brain surgeons had a problem. The bulging brain is mysterious because you get no clues to tell you what's going on inside it. I mean there's no helpful sign saying…

Unlike certain other parts of the body, the brain doesn't do interesting things like digest food, burp or even fart. The brain just sits around all day squelching to itself.

So it's not so surprising that these early pioneers made some mind-boggling mistakes.

MIND-BOGGLING MISTAKES

The ancient Egyptians and Greeks thought that the thinking part of the body was the heart. This seemed right because your heart beats faster when you're upset or excited. Is that why your teacher (who could be as old as the pyramids) makes you learn boring facts "by heart"? Well, anyway, the ancient Greeks and Egyptians were *wrong*.

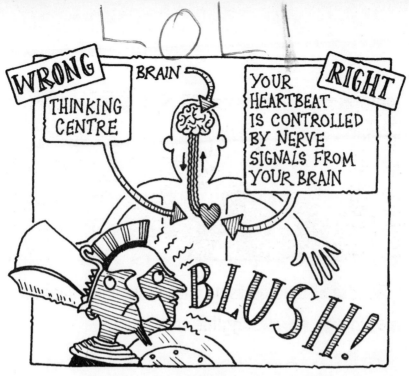

Brainy Greek philosopher Aristotle (384–322 BC) also thought the heart did the thinking. He reckoned the brain was simply a cooling system for the blood. According to Aristotle when you get a cold your cooling system overflows. (That's why snot dribbles out of your nose.)

But he was *wrong* too. Snot is made in the lining of the nose to catch germs and dust. Your nose is runny in a cold because your body is trying to flush out the germs that cause the illness.

Actually, Greek doctor Alcmaeon of Croton (6th century BC) had already figured out what the brain was up to. He cut up dead bodies and noticed that there were nerves running from the eyeballs to the brain. He also noted that patients with head injuries couldn't think clearly. "Clearly," thought Al, "the brain has to be involved in seeing and thinking."

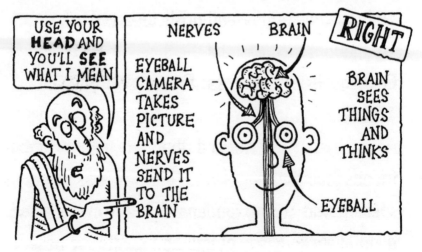

But for over 1,000 years doctors remained puzzled. They weren't sure how the brain worked or what the different bits were for. There were theories, of course. One widely held view was that you did your thinking in the fluid-filled spaces inside the brain known as ventricles (ven-trick-als). The rest of the brain was a squelchy bubble-wrap to cushion the vital holes. But by the 18th century scientists were looking at the brain in a more scientific way. And making strange and grisly discoveries…

Bulging brain secrets: Franz Gall (1758–1828)

As a child Franz noticed that one of his school friends had bulging eyes. This boy was good at spelling and Franz wondered if everyone who was good at spelling had bulging eyes. After he became a doctor in Vienna he cut up dead bodies and came to the conclusion that the eyes bulged because the brain behind them was also bulging. Franz reckoned this bulging area dealt with spelling.

Franz was convinced that the size of other brain bulges reflect your personality — for example, whether you're greedy, enjoy smashing things up or have a sense of humour. And to prove this he measured hundreds of skulls of executed criminals and tried to link the bumps he found with the criminals' known personal traits.

Despite his many skulls, er, I mean skills, Franz was on the wrong track. There is no link between the shape of your brain and your personal qualities. But up to the 1850s many people believed Franz had found a way to measure personality. And when Franz's own brain was examined after his death it was found to be smaller than average. Now, I wonder what that could mean?

The talking brain: Paul Broca (1824–1880)

Paul was working as a surgeon in Paris when he met a patient named Tan. "Tan" was his nickname because the poor man had suffered a brain injury that left him unable to speak any word except "tan". Tan was already ill when he saw Broca. Broca could do nothing to help his patient and a few days later he died.

Tan's misfortune was a great opportunity for

science. Broca cut open Tan's brain and found that the injury was in what's now imaginatively known as Broca's area (surely it ought to be called Tan's area?). Broca realized that this area of the brain helps you pronounce words properly.

This was a major discovery, but as far as speech goes it wasn't the last word – geddit? In 1874 German scientist Carl Wernicke (1848–1905) found another bit (now known – surprise, surprise – as Wernicke's area) which helps you *choose* the right words. People with brain damage in this area often talk utter drivel but with perfect grammar. (For more details see page 103.)

The twitching brain: Julius Eduard Hitzig (1838–1907)

If Mrs Hitzig had walked into the bedroom unexpectedly one day in 1870 she would have received a horrible shock. Her husband and his pal Gustav Fritsch were experimenting on a dog's brain using her dressing-table as a workbench.

At the time, Hitzig was working as a doctor in Switzerland but he didn't have a lab of his own. (By the way it's a bad idea to use your mum's dressing-table to practise your brain surgery. You could use the bathroom instead, but make sure you mop the floor afterwards.)

Actually, the dog was getting quite a shock too. An electric shock to the left side of its brain. Hitzig found that this made the dog's right legs twitch. This electrifying test proved that the left side of the brain controls the right side of the body and vice versa. Later in the year war broke out between Germany and France, and Hitzig got the chance to try the same tests on wounded soldiers with bits of their brains shot away. The results confirmed his theory.

As a result of the work of these pioneers, new groups of scientists began to take an interest in the brain. You'll be coming across some of them later on in this book. Here's a handy guide to help you spot them...

Spot the scientists

1. Neurophysiologists
(new-ro-fizzy-olo-gists)

INTERESTED IN: Finding out how the brain and nerves work.

WHAT THEY DO: Study bits of chopped-up brain and analyse chemicals from the brain.

WHERE THEY WORK: University laboratories or large hospital labs.

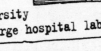

2. Neurologists (new-rol-lo-gists)

INTERESTED IN: Studying the brain and nerves, too, but they're especially keen on horrible but fascinating brain and nerve diseases.

WHAT THEY DO: Treat patients with diseases of the nerves and brain. Some of them are also neurosurgeons which is the posh term for brain surgeons.

WHERE THEY WORK: Hospitals.

3. Psychiatrists (si-ki-a-trists)

INTERESTED IN: Diseases of the mind. Psychiatrists are trained as doctors rather than purely scientists.

WHAT THEY DO: Talk to the patient and attempt to find the causes of their illness.

WHERE THEY WORK: general hospitals and psychiatric hospitals and clinics.

4. Psychologists (si-col-lo-gists)

INTERESTED IN: Studying the brain by looking at the way it makes people behave.

FASCINATING!

WHAT THEY DO: Set up experiments to find out how people react in certain situations. Some of these tests are a bit wacky. Some psychologists are interested in diseases of the mind, but unlike psychiatrists they are not trained as doctors.

WHERE THEY WORK: University labs and hospitals.

PECULIAR PSYCHOLOGISTS

The psychologists take their lead from a very peculiar German scientist, and here's his story…

Hall of fame: Gustav Fechner (1801–1887)
Nationality: German

Fechner's brain was always bulging with ideas but his interest in the mind began with a horrible accident. The physics professor was studying light when he blinded himself by looking at the sun. (Something you should never do.) So you could say poor old Gus got blinded by science – geddit. He became so miserable that he went mad for two years.

But one day he was sitting in the garden and he felt a sudden impulse to tear off his bandages. Amazingly, he found he could see again! Incredible colours flooded his brain and he was so excited he imagined he could see brains inside flowers. (Yes, you did read that last bit correctly.) Gus wrote a peculiar book describing how plants have minds. (Believe this and you're a real cabbage-brain.)

Two years later Gus was enjoying a lie-in. Well, maybe "enjoying" is the wrong word. Gus was racking his brains. And not about whether he'd find a toy in his packet of breakfast cereal or how to make contact with a turnip. He was trying to think of a way to study the brain using scientific experiments rather than cutting it open on an operating table. Then he had a brainwave.

All you had to do was measure how the brain reacts to different sensations. For example, in one test Gus shone a light in a volunteer's eyes and slowly increased the brightness until they noticed the change. This allowed him to measure the brain's ability to notice changes in brightness.

Gus had launched a new branch of science called psychology – the study of human behaviour (although the name actually means "study of the mind" in Greek). And this exciting new science owed its existence to the fact that the scientist fancied an extra snooze. (Tell your parents this story next time you want a lie-in, you never know they might even fall for it.)

Fechner's work was continued by German Wilhelm Wundt (1832–1920), who set up the world's first psychology lab. Wundt never laughed or smiled or joked and spent his entire life working.

SORRY READERS, NO JOKES ALLOWED WITH THIS PICTURE

His books totalled 53,735 pages – that's equal to writing a 500-page book every year for 100 years. He wrote so much that critics complained that it was hard to discover what Wundt actually thought. American psychologist George A Miller wrote…

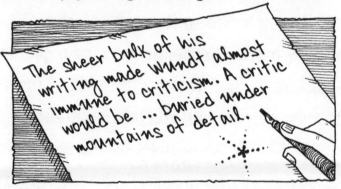

The sheer bulk of his writing made Wundt almost immune to criticism. A critic would be … buried under mountains of detail.

Brilliant, eh? So if you want to baffle your teacher write a 500-page essay for your science homework. But this tactic didn't stop other psychologists disagreeing with Wundt's approach to psychology. Increasingly they were finding that the brain did a lot more than simply respond to sensations.

Another German psychologist Max Wertheimer (1880–1943) wondered if the brain plays tricks to help make sense of a film. A film is made up of thousands of pictures that you see very quickly – about 24 pictures a second. The brain can't keep up with this rapid change so it sees the pictures as a continuously moving scene. So your brain gets the whole picture – and you get the whole movie, including the exciting bits *and* the happy ending.

Max dreamt up this idea on a train in 1910. He was supposed to be on holiday but he excitedly leapt off the train (he waited for it to stop first – he wasn't that excited) and set up experiments to find out why.

Max proved the brain sees the whole scene first and then figures out how the moving objects relate to one another. And he worked out a new theory of psychology called Gestalt (ge-shtal-t) based on these ideas. The new theory underlined the importance of finding out how the brain makes sense of things like the film. This was a step forward from Wundt's work, which simply looked at how the brain responds to sensations.

Meanwhile American psychologists such as John B. Watson (1878–1958) and, later, Burrhus Skinner (1904–1990) were changing the behaviour of rats by training their brains. (You can read more about Watson and his wacky experiments on page 114.)

BULGING BRAIN EXPRESSIONS

Two brain surgeons are quarrelling…

Is the quarrel about gardening?

ANSWER

No. The amygdala (a-mig-dal-a) and putumen (putt-you-men) – almond and fruit stone in Greek – are odd names for areas of the brain.

Confused yet? Well, there are lots more bits and pieces you'll need to know about if you're going to be a brain surgeon. Maybe things would be clearer if you could get your hands on a real dripping brain. Fancy a squidge? Hope so, if not the next chapter's so nasty, it could drive you out of your mind.

Better sharpen that scalpel…

BULGING BRAIN BITS 'N' PIECES

As a brain surgeon you need to know all about the main bits and pieces in the brain. Fortunately we've got hold of a real genuine brain from a real genuinely dead person to help you. Go on, take a peek – it won't bite you.

BRAIN BITS AND PIECES

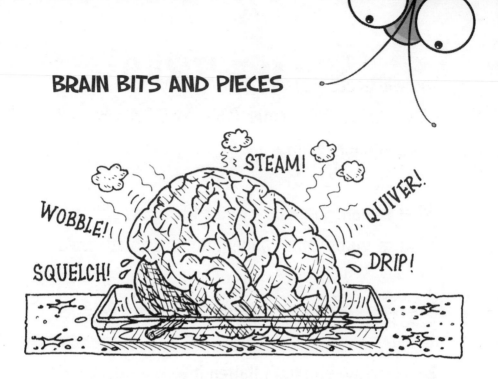

WOBBLE!

STEAM!

QUIVER!

SQUELCH!

DRIP!

The main area you can see is the cortex (that's the wrinkly, thinking bit, remember?).

DARE YOU DISCOVER ... WHY THE CORTEX IS WRINKLY?

Ever wondered why brains are wrinkly? Now's your chance to discover the *real* answer...

You will need:

• Two sheets of A4 paper. (Your school report might come in handy here.)

What you do:

1 Screw one sheet of paper into a tight little ball.

2 Open it up but don't flatten it.

3 Place it over the second sheet of A4 paper.

What do you notice?

a) The screwed-up paper seems to have shrunk.

b) The screwed-up paper has got bigger.

c) Both sheets of paper are the same size.

a) The wrinkles and bumps on the paper make it take up less space. The wrinkles on your cortex allow a larger area to squash between your ears. And that's very important because the cortex is very thin – no more than 3 mm (0.12 inches) thick. If your brain was flat it would be the size of a pillowcase and you'd need a huge head to contain it.

To find out more about some of the vital brain bits and pieces let's have a peek at this gory but fascinating medical textbook.

Brain Surgery for Beginners

Chapter 1: Brain bits and pieces

Cerebrum (ser-ree-brum)

This is the largest bit of the brain – it's so big it makes up 85 per cent of the brain. This area is REALLY important because its wrinkly surface is the cortex, where thinking takes place. The cerebrum is divided into two halves (no one knows the reason for the split). The halves are linked by a bridge at the base made of millions of nerve cells.

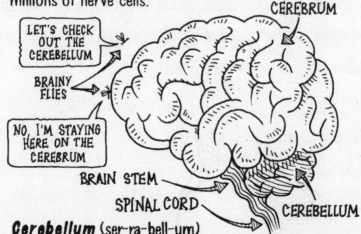

CEREBRUM

LET'S CHECK OUT THE CEREBELLUM

BRAINY FLIES

NO, I'M STAYING HERE ON THE CEREBRUM

BRAIN STEM

SPINAL CORD

CEREBELLUM

Cerebellum (ser-ra-bell-um)

The name means "little brain" in Latin – because it looks a bit like a little brain. This pear-sized blob has two halves – one for each side of the brain. Both sides help the brain balance and control its body's movements.

BET YOU NEVER KNEW!

When you learn a skill such as riding a bike you think about what you're doing. Well, hopefully – otherwise you'd fall off. But after a while you happily pedal around without thinking. Oh, so you knew that? Well, when you stop thinking about what you're doing your cerebellum takes over from your thinking cortex and tells your body what to do. Scientists have found that with the cerebellum in charge you can move faster and less clumsily. (For more details on what the cerebellum can do check out page 103 and page 132)

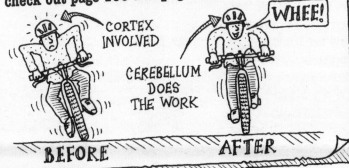

CORTEX INVOLVED

CEREBELLUM DOES THE WORK

WHEE!

BEFORE   AFTER

Spinal cord

This is a bundle of nerves about 45 cm long and as thick as a thumb. Although it's not part of the brain, as a brain surgeon you need to know what it does. It actually takes signals to and from the brain.

Brain stem

This bit links the brain with the spinal cord. It's useful for helping the brain to go to sleep. And it's also useful for waking up the brain to danger or something interesting.

As a brain surgeon you'll need to know a bit more about the even smaller but still vital bits and pieces that lurk deep within the brain. We've cut some brains in half to help you...

Thalamus

Scientists are still finding out what this bit does. You've actually got a pair of them – one for each side of your brain. Each thalamus is packed with neurons and seems to work like a switchboard, routing nerve signals from all your senses except smell to your cortex. It also passes on messages from the cortex to do with moving your muscles and helps to control levels of brain activity. So it probably shuts down in science lessons.

PINEAL GLAND HYPOTHALAMUS
PITUITARY GLAND

half a brain (side view)

Hypothalamus (hi-po-thal-a-mus)

A bossy little blob the size of one of your knuckles. It reckons *it's* the boss of the entire body. Controls the water content in the blood, its temperature, sweating, shivering, growing, when you sleep, etc.

The pituitary gland

Vital sidekick for the hypothalamus. Follows its orders and makes the chemicals that go round in the blood. These chemicals, or hormones as scientists call them, order the body to do what the hypothalamus wants.

47

The pineal (pi-nee-al) gland

The pineal gland is linked to your eyes and is sensitive to light and dark. In the dark it makes a substance that stops children from developing into adults too early. You may also like to know there's a fish called a lamprey that has a pineal like an extra eye on top of its head. The extra eye gives it all-round vision. (Scientists have failed to prove the common belief that teachers have this eye in the back of their heads.)

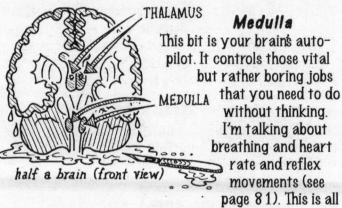

THALAMUS

MEDULLA

half a brain (front view)

Medulla

This bit is your brain's auto-pilot. It controls those vital but rather boring jobs that you need to do without thinking. I'm talking about breathing and heart rate and reflex movements (see page 81). This is all very handy and your mighty medulla also makes you vomit which isn't quite as nice. Mind you, this can be vital if you've eaten some poison or a school dinner.

Limbic (lim-bick) system

An odd mixture of bits and pieces including the amygdala (known in English as the "almond") and hypothamus deep in the brain. Shapes your feelings and also involved in memory.

WHOOPS! ER, FANCY AN ALMOND SLICE, NURSE?

BRAIN SURGERY FOR BEGINNERS

Chapter 2: Vital brain tests

Of course, as a brain surgeon you'll be performing operations on living patients (hopefully they'll still be alive after the operation too).

DON'T WORRY, I'VE READ A BOOK ABOUT IT!

To help you plan your operations there is an amazing collection of machines that can show what's going on inside the brain before you get cutting. This is useful because you can find out which areas may be damaged or not functioning properly. Let's check them out ...

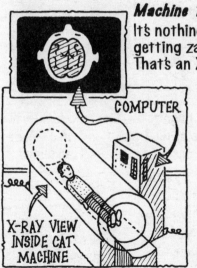

COMPUTER

X-RAY VIEW INSIDE CAT MACHINE

Machine 1: an X-ray CT
It's nothing to do with a puss getting zapped by radiation. That's an X-ray CAT.

CT means computerised tomography (toe-mog-graf-ee). Well, you need to spout the jargon effortlessly if you're a brain surgeon. The machine sends weak X-rays through the brain and shows up the result on a computer screen.

These days it's often used with other machines such as ...

Machine 2: a PET

You don't need cat food for this pet — it's a Positive Emission Tomography (poz-it-tiv e-miss-e-on toe-mog-graf-ee) machine. Your poor old patient has to be injected with a radioactive chemical. The scanner detects what happens when the blood takes the chemical into their brain. The blood flows to the bits of the brain that are most active. So you can see what's going on and spot any areas that don't seem to be working properly.

Machine 3: a MRI means Magnetic Resonance Imaging

This is the high-tech gizmo you really want to get your surgical gloves on. It surrounds the brain with magnetic force and zaps the brain with radio waves. The machine detects radio waves bouncing back from hydrogen atoms in the brain (hydrogen is an ingredient of water so there are billions of hydrogen atoms in your brain). The scanner turns the signals into a cool picture of slices of brain and even shows where blood is flowing. And since a brain bit gets more blood when it's busy, it can show which brain bits are used for jobs such as talking or making a chewing gum sculpture.

Machine 4: an EEG

This stands for electroencephalograph (el-leck-tro-en-cef-falo-graf) machine. The metal electrodes pick up electrical signals given off as the brain thinks and the machine displays them as a print-out showing the signals as peaks.

Important note to the reader:

Sorry to interrupt the book. Just a quick message to say that the EEG machine is an ultra-sensitive piece of equipment. This was tested by an American doctor in the mid-1970s who wired up a lime-flavoured jelly to an EEG machine. (The flavour didn't actually affect the test.) According to the machine, the jelly was alive and thinking! In fact, it was reacting to people chatting in the next room. So make sure you read this book q-u-i-e-t-l-y.

Checking the print out

Here's what your EEG print out might show.

1 An alpha rhythm. This means the brain's thinking in a dreamy kind of way.

2 Beta rhythm (a bit faster). The brain is paying attention to what's going on.

3 Theta rhythm (a bit slower). The brain is feeling sleepy.

4 Delta rhythm (very slow). The brain has fallen into a deep sleep. (This has been found to be a common condition amongst children in science lessons.)

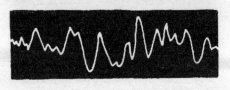

If the line is completely flat you should check that your patient is still alive. A flat line normally means the patient is dead!

BET YOU NEVER KNEW!

The EEG was invented by German Dr Hans Berger (1873-1941) who spent five years sticking electrodes on people's heads to measure brain activity. He even tested his invention on his children. Hans reckoned he would be able to show what his children and the other patients were thinking. He couldn't do this but he spent another five years writing up his experiments. And then ... no one took any notice.

It wasn't until British scientist Edgar Adrian (1889–1977) showed that unusual wave patterns could be a sign of brain disease that EEG machines were used in hospitals.

BRAIN SURGERY FOR BEGINNERS

Chapter 3: Surgical tools

Congratulations, you're now almost ready for your first brain operation! First, though, you need to get familiar with a few brain surgeon's tools.

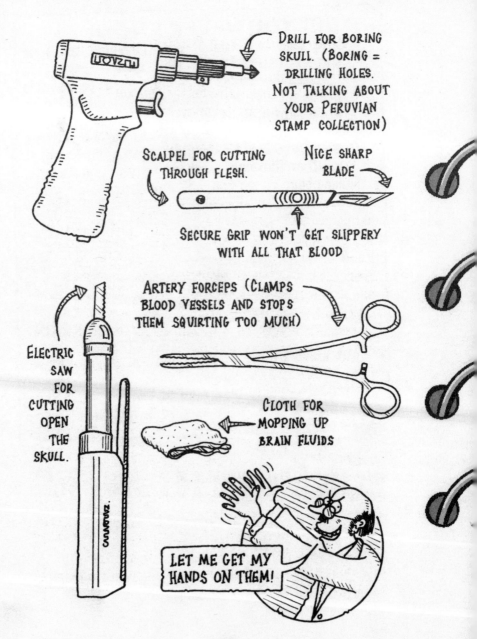

DRILL FOR BORING SKULL. (BORING = DRILLING HOLES. NOT TALKING ABOUT YOUR PERUVIAN STAMP COLLECTION)

SCALPEL FOR CUTTING THROUGH FLESH.

NICE SHARP BLADE

SECURE GRIP WON'T GET SLIPPERY WITH ALL THAT BLOOD

ARTERY FORCEPS (CLAMPS BLOOD VESSELS AND STOPS THEM SQUIRTING TOO MUCH)

ELECTRIC SAW FOR CUTTING OPEN THE SKULL.

CLOTH FOR MOPPING UP BRAIN FLUIDS

LET ME GET MY HANDS ON THEM!

54

Chapter 4: Your first operation

Just before you move on to the surgery bit, take a look at these handy instructions. Better still, keep them by your side during the actual operation.

Brain surgery instructions

1 It helps if you have a particular operation in mind before you begin. For example you might want to remove a blood clot or a fragment of bone after an accident. No responsible brain surgeon would cut open someone's brain just to take a peek inside.

2 Use a PET or MRI scan to help you plan where to cut. In 1998, scientists at Toronto Hospital developed an MRI scanner that you can use to guide your scalpel whilst actually operating.

3 Make sure there are no germs in the area of your operation. It's not enough to clear away the tea things and put the cat out. The entire area should be scrubbed with strong disinfectant to kill germs. You should be thoroughly washed and wear a face mask and a specially disinfected gown.

4 Draw a line on the patient's head to show where you intend to cut. Oops! Nearly forgot. The patient's head should be shaven to prevent bits of hair getting mixed in with their brain.

5 To get at the brain you need to remove a bit of skull. First drill some holes in the skull. (You'll have to concentrate. One slip and you might drill through the brain.)

6 Next, saw between the holes and lift up a flap of skull and meninges (men-in-gees) – the protective layers under the skull. As you lift the meninges you may hear a *sclurping* noise as the clear fluid that surrounds the brain bubbles out.

7 If everything goes according to plan the brain should be pulsing as the blood squirts through its blood vessels.

8 Now to begin your brilliant brain operation...

HORRIBLE HEALTH WARNING!

Stop! Don't do anything until
you've read the next page!

IMPORTANT AND VERY URGENT ANNOUNCEMENT:

In order to do brain surgery properly you have to study in medical school for at least seven years. You didn't really think you'd be allowed to do brain surgery at your age did you? Sorry to disappoint you. You'd better stick everything back together and be grateful. Why? Because practising brain surgery without proper training could land you in serious legal trouble and result in your pocket money being stopped for 33,000,000 years. Sorry!

Still, there's lots more fascinating things to find out about the brain. For example, there are the amazing ways in which it manages to find out what's going on around you. These are called "senses". So here's a challenge for your brain – has it got the sense to read the next chapter? Better find out!

STARTLING SENSES

Without senses life would be like sitting in a dark cupboard. Yep, even more boring than watching a TV in a power cut. But thanks to your senses you are bombarded with startling sights and sounds and smells. So it's lucky you've got strong nerves – after all, your senses won't work without nerves...

Bulging brains fact file

Name: Nerves

Basic facts:

1 A network of nerves spreads from your brain and your spinal cord to reach every nook and cranny of your body. Their job is to carry signals from your senses to your brain and orders from your brain to get those lazy muscles moving.

2 In all you have over 72 km of nerves in your body. No wonder you feel a bundle of nerves at times!

3 An average-sized nerve is made up of thousands of neurons.

Disgusting details:

1 Your nerves are always keyed up and ready for action. In fact, when they send a signal they actually stop working! (See next page for details.)

2 So it's more relaxing for your nerves when you do something than when you laze around all day doing nothing!

Your nerves are a bit like an amazing telephone system that takes messages all around your body. Just imagine they were a phone system – the manual would make fascinating reading…

HOW TO USE NEURO-PHONE

You'll always get the message with Neuro-phone!

Congratulations on buying Neuro-phone, the high-tech intra-bodily communication network! Each neuron wire is custom built to send speedy and reliable messages ten times faster than a champion sprinter! Now you can move your body, waggle your ears or slurp a milkshake! Just do what you feel like!

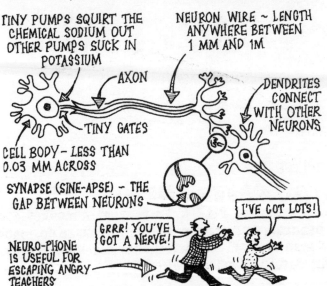

TINY PUMPS SQUIRT THE CHEMICAL SODIUM OUT OTHER PUMPS SUCK IN POTASSIUM

NEURON WIRE ~ LENGTH ANYWHERE BETWEEN 1 MM AND 1M

AXON

DENDRITES CONNECT WITH OTHER NEURONS

TINY GATES

CELL BODY - LESS THAN 0.03 MM ACROSS

SYNAPSE (SINE-APSE) - THE GAP BETWEEN NEURONS

I'VE GOT LOTS!

GRRR! YOU'VE GOT A NERVE!

NEURO-PHONE IS USEFUL FOR ESCAPING ANGRY TEACHERS

To activate your Neuro-phone system you don't need to worry about boring dialling codes or numbers. Simply ask your brain cortex to send a message anywhere you want in the body. Neuro-phone will do the rest for you. . . here's how.

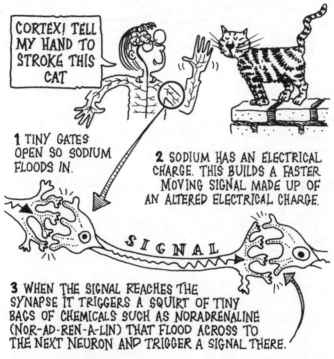

CORTEX! TELL MY HAND TO STROKE THIS CAT

1 TINY GATES OPEN SO SODIUM FLOODS IN.

2 SODIUM HAS AN ELECTRICAL CHARGE. THIS BUILDS A FASTER MOVING SIGNAL MADE UP OF AN ALTERED ELECTRICAL CHARGE.

SIGNAL

3 WHEN THE SIGNAL REACHES THE SYNAPSE IT TRIGGERS A SQUIRT OF TINY BAGS OF CHEMICALS SUCH AS NORADRENALINE (NOR-AD-REN-A-LIN) THAT FLOOD ACROSS TO THE NEXT NEURON AND TRIGGER A SIGNAL THERE.

BET YOU NEVER KNEW!

1 Nerve signals are F-A-S-T. Tests show a monkey can spot a banana, use its cortex to decide what to do, reach out and grab the food – all within one second. Could you move any faster if someone offered you a choccie?

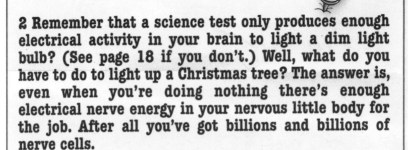

2 Remember that a science test only produces enough electrical activity in your brain to light a dim light bulb? (See page 18 if you don't.) Well, what do you have to do to light up a Christmas tree? The answer is, even when you're doing nothing there's enough electrical nerve energy in your nervous little body for the job. After all you've got billions and billions of nerve cells.

SENSATIONAL SENSES

Thanks to your sensational senses you can appreciate the true beauty of the world. A lovely blue cloudless sky, the delicious aroma of new-baked pizza and the soft smooth touch of velvet…

Let's take a closer look at these marvellous abilities…

BULGING BRAIN EXPRESSIONS

Some psychologists are chatting over dinner…

MY ANOSMIA IS REALLY BAD

YOU'RE LUCKY IT ISN'T PAROSMIA

Are these weird types of food?

ANSWER

No. These are problems caused by blows on the head.
Anosmia = you can't smell anything.
Parosmia = all food tastes disgusting. Of course the scientists might have been eating a school dinner. Then their food would have tasted truly terrible!

BET YOU NEVER KNEW!

The sense of taste gets weaker as we grow older. At present scientists don't understand why this happens, but you can observe the effects any lunchtime. Many children can't stand the vile flavour of school dinners but elderly teachers happily relish the revolting recipes.

DARE YOU DISCOVER ... A TOUCH OF THE RIDICULOUS?

You will need:

• Your body

• Clothes (don't forget to put some on your body)

What you do:

1 Nothing. If only all science experiments were this easy!

2 Concentrate on trying to feel the clothes you are wearing against your skin. (Don't touch them with your hands.)

What do you notice?

a) I can't feel anything except my itchy socks.

b) I can feel the material against my skin. Funny I never noticed it before.

c) This experiment has given me a headache.

ANSWER

b) If your nerves feel a constant sensation like your clothes they get used to it and stop firing. That's why you don't feel your clothes and you may forget you're wearing any. Hopefully, you should notice if you're not wearing any.

If **c)** stop concentrating so hard and if **a)** consider the possibility that you're only wearing your socks. This could be a sight for sore eyes, and talking about vision…

SEEING IS BELIEVING

You might think that you see with your eyes. But your eyeballs simply act like cameras and pick up light patterns from the outside world. It's the brain that makes sense of this information. Sounds complicated? Well, fortunately, the Neuro-phone people have logged the neuron calls involved so you can make sense of it all.

Take a look at this…

You see through your eyeballs. An image of the scene falls on the retina and the one million neurons in your optic nerve take the image in the form of nerve pulses to your brain. Now read on…

1 Retina to thalamus, "GET A LOOK AT THIS!"

RETINA

THALAMUS

2 Thalamus to vision centre at back of cortex, "SOMETHING'S UP. WANNA TAKE A PEEK?"

CORTEX VISION CENTRE

EYEBALL LENS

CHOCCIES

3 Cortex to eyeball muscles, "MOVE THAT EYEBALL ROUND. I WANT A BETTER LOOK"

4 Cortex to eyeball lens muscles, "CAN YOU FOCUS A TEENY BIT MORE?"

5 Meanwhile in the vision centre of the cortex the neurons are chatting away and making sense of what you see...

EYEBALL MUSCLES

LENS MUSCLES

"HEY, SHAPE DEPARTMENT – CAN YOU CHECK OUT THAT SHAPE?"
"LOOKS LIKE A BOX OF CHOCCIES TO ME."

"COLOUR DEPARTMENT – ANY NEWS?"
"IT'S DEFINITELY PINK."

"MOVEMENT DEPARTMENT – ANY ACTION?"
"NOPE – IT'S JUST SITTING THERE."

A message to the reader:

Yep, this is really true. Everything you look at, including this page and these words, is seen *inside* your brain. You also need your brain to make sense of the words (see page 109 for details).

BET YOU NEVER KNEW!

Imagine you're in a science test. At times like this you're concentrating so hard your brain blots out your vision from the corner of your eyes. You also stop hearing background noises because your brain blots these out so you can concentrate on the job you are doing. Scientists aren't sure how your brain performs this useful trick. But without it you'd fail the test and there'd be a terrible blot on your school record.

COULD YOU BE A SCIENTIST?

Scientists at Vanderbilt University, USA, tested some children. The children were blindfolded and given a heap of smelly old T-shirts to sniff. They were asked to spot the distinctive pong of T-shirts belonging to their brothers or sisters. How do you think they got on?

a) The experiment had to be stopped after the horrible stink made some of the children throw up.

b) The children could easily recognize the pong made by their brothers and sisters. They got over 75 per cent of the tests right.

OH WHAT A HIDEOUSLY GROSS PONG!

HANG ON, WE HAVEN'T STARTED YET

c) The children found it impossible to identify the smell made by their brothers and sisters.

b) And in tests 16 out of 18 parents could identify their children by their smell. Your sense of smell is better than you may imagine. If you lie on the floor you can actually detect the cheesy pong where someone in a dirty sock walked on the floorboards.

(No need to test this remarkable skill just now.) And you can identify over 10,000 different whiffs and stinks. (Heaven nose how you do it!)

BRINGING IT ALL TOGETHER

Of course in everyday life your brain uses all your senses together to build up a picture of what's going on outside your head. Maybe you'd like to discover how it all slots together. Your mission, should you choose to accept it is to … (BIG ROLL OF DRUMS HERE) … eat a chocolate.

(Yep, but it's not as simple it sounds.) Before we start let's listen into those Neuro-phone messages and get an idea of what's involved.

JUST A BITE

Retina to vision centre and brain stem, "I CAN'T TAKE MY EYES OFF THOSE CHOCOLATES."

Brain stem to cortex, "THERE'S SOMETHING INTERESTING AHEAD. WANNA CHECK IT OUT?"

Cortex to fingers and arms, "EXTEND FINGERS AND PICK UP A CHOCOLATE. HOW DOES IT FEEL?"

Finger-touch receptors to thalamus, "TELL THE CORTEX IT'S LOVELY AND COOL AND SMOOTH AND VELVETY."

Thalamus to sensory area of cortex, "YOU GOT ALL THAT?"

Ears to medulla, "HEY, LISTEN TO THAT LOVELY RUSTLE IN THE BOX."

Medulla to thalamus, "PSST! TELL THE CORTEX TO GET A LOAD OF THIS."

Nose to thalamus, "WOW! WHAT A LOVELY CHOCOLATEY WHIFF - TELL THE CORTEX TO GET A SNIFF OF THIS."

Tongue to cortex, "I'M READY TO SWALLOW. THERE'S LOADS OF SPIT DOWN HERE!"

A note to the reader:

Drooling spit at the sight of a choccie is a reflex (see page 81), triggered by nerves leading from the brain to your gooey saliva glands. Are you starting to drool too? If so, try not to dribble on the nice clean page.

Another note to the reader:

So do you fancy trying this mission for yourself? Chances are you've already had quite a bit of practice. But if you feel like checking whether your brain can handle all these senses it's worth asking your parents for chocolates. You could explain that you need an extra large box in order to get this vital science experiment absolutely right. And if your parents fall for that, you might as well ask for a day out at a theme park, too.

So how did you get on...?

a) I ate the chocolate so fast I didn't have a chance to follow the instructions.

b) I got muddled up with the instructions and bit my tongue by mistake. Ouch!

c) It was great and all my senses and brain bits worked perfectly.

(If you chose **a)**: oh dear, that's tough, better practise on another choccie. If **b)**: you might as well go on to the next section. Because it's a bit of a PAIN too.)

PUTTING UP WITH PAIN

Pain is the worst thing you can sense. But you know all about pain already…

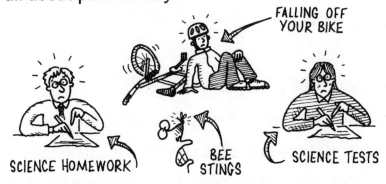

FALLING OFF YOUR BIKE

SCIENCE HOMEWORK

BEE STINGS

SCIENCE TESTS

DARE YOU DISCOVER … HOW TO PUT UP WITH PAIN?

Note to the reader:
This experiment has been banned on the grounds that it's far too cruel. Here are a few facts instead.

A FEW PAINFUL FACTS

1 Pain is a big trick played by your bulging brain on the rest of your body. Imagine you stub your toe on a stone or even the cat.

You might think you feel the resulting pain in your big toe. But you actually experience the pain in your brain because that's where the nerve signal goes.

2 Your body is crowded with countless thousands of pain receptors. Obviously any damage to the body is red-hot urgent news for the brain – there may be more damage just about to occur so the pain receptors try to let the brain know what's going on NOW.

3 So the pain receptors fire off high-speed nerve signals to blast your brain. It's hard to ignore them – isn't it?

4 The deeper the pain receptors, the less sensitive they are – that's why a really bad injury can hurt less than a little scratch. Pain deep in the body often feels like a dull miserable ache.

5 Different pain signals move at different speeds. A sharp prick on your skin hits your brain at 29.9 metres a second. A longer pulse like a burning or aching pain moves through the neurons at a slightly more leisurely 1.98 metres a second.

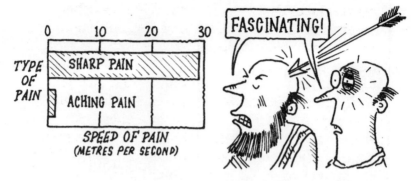

But there's much more to pain than just a horrible feeling in the brain. Here, for a change, is a bit of good news...

THE DAILY BRAIN

The paper that makes you think!   Issue 3,752 . 1975

What a relief!

Scientists at Aberdeen University, Scotland, claim brains help deaden pain. Brain researchers John Hughes and Hans Kosterlitz were following a lead from neurophysiologists in Baltimore, USA. Now they reckon they've found what they were after. Previously unknown chemicals called enkephalins (en-kefa-lins) that block pain signals. Meanwhile US scientists have found more **pain-blocking** chemicals called endorphins in the brain and nerves. They sound like a real painless discovery!

Daily Brain Science Correspondent Dr Alan de Mind writes... The newly discovered chemicals may explain why taking exercise or other distractions such as a white knuckle ride or an exciting film takes your mind off pain. Presumably doing these things can trigger the brain to make the painkilling chemicals.

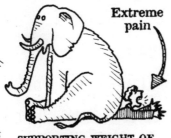

Extreme pain

SUPPORTING WEIGHT OF ELEPHANT WITHOUT ENKEPHALINS

Extremely exciting film

SUPPORTING WEIGHT OF ELEPHANT WITH ENKEPHALINS

BET YOU NEVER KNEW!

Another way to deaden pain is to confuse your nerves by getting them to send other signals. So if you bang your shin you could try rubbing it with your hand or a lump of ice. This gets the nerves sending more signals that swamp the pain signals.

THE PAINFUL TRUTH

Afterwards it's hard to remember exactly what pain is like. Your cruel heartless brain wants every pain you feel to seem really awful and unexpected. That way you'll do something about it. The painful truth is that pain is there so your brain can teach you a painful lesson.

You might think it would be lovely to live in a world without pain. Life would be brilliant, wouldn't it? You could wander around endlessly bumping into things, and not worrying about how much it was going to hurt. Until one day you noticed that your fingers had dropped off. Of course, if you'd felt pain in the first place you'd have got away with a nasty cut rather than no fingers on one hand.

By the way, if the thought of all that blood makes you feel like throwing up at this point feel free –

being sick, or vomiting to use the technical term, is just another of your…

ACTION-PACKED REFLEXES

Do you do things without thinking? If your answer is "yeah, all the time" then you've probably been making a few reflex actions. Reflexes are actions that your body does in response to startling signals from your senses. These are things like sneezing and coughing and dribbling that you can't stop once they start. (For this reason farting or burping are not reflexes and you've got no excuse for doing them during mealtimes.)

REFLEX ACTION — ATCHOO! REFLEX ACTION — COUGH! REFLEX ACTION — DRIBBLE! DISGUSTING HABIT — BURP!

A few more facts you ought to know about reflexes

1 Your brain isn't involved in reflexes. The signals go to your spinal cord and out again in nerves that control your muscles. This saves time and means that you can whip your hand away from the hot plate of the cooker in 0.03 seconds instead of up to 0.8 seconds if your brain was consulted.

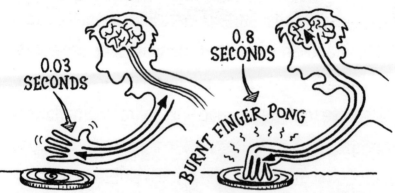

2 Some of the most important work about reflexes was carried out by Russian Ivan Pavlov (1849–1936). Pavlov was a cold unfriendly man who flew into terrible rages if anyone dared criticize him. And no, he wasn't a teacher, he was a scientist.

3 His most famous experiment was to show that you could train dogs to make reflex actions. Dogs dribble when they see food. Pavlov rang a bell every time the dogs were fed. After a while he stopped feeding the dogs but they still dribbled when he rang the bell.

4 Pavlov was so keen on scientific accuracy that he even measured the amount of spit the dogs dribbled.

This added no particular value to his work but it showed how seriously he took his job. Would you want a job measuring dog's dribble? If you think it's a mouth-watering opportunity you're a born scientist.

DARE YOU DISCOVER ... A REFLEX ACTION?

You will need:
- One dog (count first to make sure it's got four legs)

What you do:
1 Rub the dog's back until the dog reacts.
2 Note what happens next.

What happens next?
a) The dog falls over.

b) The dog scratches its back with its hind legs. (It probably thinks your hand is an extra large flea.)

c) The dog wags its tail and sticks its tongue out and dribbles everywhere.

ANSWER

b) The dog often scratches its back without thinking in a reflex action – much like you sneezing. The nerves involved in the dog's reflex were discovered by British scientist Sir Charles Sherrington (1857–1952) who won the Nobel Prize for this breakthrough. I expect he was itching to tell his pals about it – ha-ha. If **a)** your dog is probably missing a leg or two.

HORRIBLE HEALTH WARNING!

Don't try the above experiment with the neighbour's Rottweiler or you may never tie your own shoelaces again.

CONGRATULATIONS! You've successfully read this chapter. Now for the bad news. So far you've been looking at the easy-peasy stuff your brain gets up to. You might find the next chapter rather more mind-bending.

Yep – it's time to put your bulging brain to work.

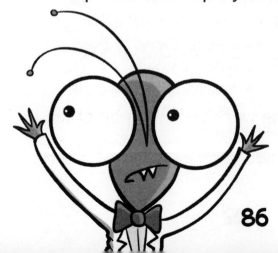

86

BULGING BRAIN-WORK

Sometimes you need your bulging brain for something more intelligent than scoffing a choccie. Jobs like listening to music, and thinking and talking and reading. Oh, so you don't think they sound too difficult? Well, they are. But don't worry, by the time you've read this chapter you'll have boosted your bulging brainpower. Well, maybe — just a bit.

FIRST SORT YOUR LEFT FROM YOUR RIGHT

Your cortex (that's the wrinkly, thinking bit of the brain, remember) is split into two halves. To understand how you use your brain you first need to know how the two halves work together. Bear in mind that one side of the cortex is stronger than the other and takes over most of the work. But which side is that? Well, the diagram below will help you sort that out. But don't forget that the left side of the cortex looks after the right side of the body and vice versa. Got all that?

Anyway, here's the diagram...

X-RAY OF SCIENCE TEACHER'S HEAD

LEFT SIDE OF BRAIN IS IN CONTROL

PEN IN RIGHT HAND

(If the teacher was left-handed these arrangements would be reversed.)

ARE YOU AMBIDEXTROUS?

Ambidextrous means that you're able to write or draw or hold a tennis racquet or play the guitar or pluck a chicken equally well with both hands.

PLAYING, ER, I MEAN PLUCKING A CHICKEN RIGHT-HANDED AND PLUCKING, OR RATHER PLAYING A GUITAR LEFT-HANDED

This is because neither side of the cortex is stronger than the other. Famous ambidextrous people include English artist Sir Edwin Landseer (1802–1873) who often drew a horse with his right hand and a stag with his left hand at the same time. Try it for yourself – it's much harder than it sounds.

TEST YOUR TEACHER

Is your teacher left-handed, right-handed or ambidextrous? Well, this teacher-teasing test will certainly keep her brain fully occupied until the end of the class. By the way, if you're feeling kind you can give your teacher one clue before you start the test: all the answers are for right-handed people.

1 Are babies always…
a) Left-handed?
b) Right-handed?
c) Ambidextrous?

2 Which side of your brain do you use for working out hard maths questions?
a) The left.
b) The right.
c) Neither, I use a calculator.

3 Which side of your brain do you use for having a chat with your friends?
a) The left.
b) The right.

c) The left for chatting with friends but the right when talking to important people like the Head Teacher.

4 Which part of your brain do you use for painting a watercolour?
a) The left.
b) The right.
c) Neither, it's the cerebellum that does the work.

I USE THE WHOLE BRAIN - IT MAKES NICE PATTERNS

5 How do Japanese people differ from the usual right—left division of work within the brain?
a) They use both sides of their brains for talking.
b) Annoying insect sounds trigger brain activity on the left side of their brains instead of the right for everyone else.
c) They can talk aloud without their brains showing unusual activity.

ANSWERS

1 c) In babies, both halves of the cortex are equally strong. One side doesn't take over until the child is about two.

2 a) If you're right-handed you read, write and work out sums mostly using the left part of your brain. (If you're left-handed you are more likely to use the right side of your brain for these tasks.)

3 a) The left side also deals with talking aloud. The poor old right side has to spend its life listening to the left side nattering.

4 b) At least the right side of the brain gets to deal with all the enjoyable artistic jobs like making a collage or drawing.

5 b) This finding was reported by Japanese scientist Tsunoda Tadanobu. Some Japanese words sound like insect or water sounds. So the scientist suggested Japanese people listen to these sounds with the left side of their brains that normally deals with language. (Award your teacher an extra mark if they managed to explain this theory.)

BET YOU NEVER KNEW!

For reasons that scientists don't quite understand...
You see things at the back of your cortex (not at the front, which is where your eyes are). You see things to the left in the right side of your brain.
Things to the right get seen in the left side.

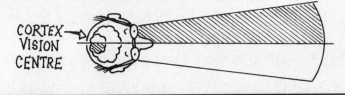

CORTEX
VISION
CENTRE

DARE YOU DISCOVER ... IF YOU'RE LEFT- OR RIGHT- EYED?

Your left eye is controlled by the right side of your brain and vice-versa. But which side of your brain is stronger? Here's how to find out...

You will need:

- A finger (preferably one of your own)
- Two eyes (these should definitely be your own)
- A stationary object 1 metre away (it doesn't

matter what this object is. It could be a picture, the wallpaper or even a dead wombat)

• A ruler

What you do:

1 Stick your finger 12 cm in front of your nose.

2 Focus your eyes on the stationary object. The finger should appear out of focus. Note the position of the finger.

3 Now wink each of your eyes in turn.

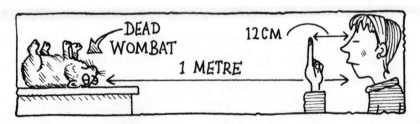

What do you notice?

a) Nothing and people started asking me whom I was winking at. It was all very embarrassing.

b) Each time I winked an eye the finger seemed to jump sideways.

c) The finger seemed to stay where it was when I winked one eye and jump sideways when I winked the other.

ANSWER

c) The finger didn't appear to move when you looked at it through your dominant eye. This is because with both eyes open you see mostly through that eye. Right-handed people usually have a dominant right eye and so they do most of their seeing in the left-hand side of their brains. OK, got all that? Here's a chance to rest your eyes for a bit and listen to some music.

COULD YOU BE A SCIENTIST?

When you listen to music the following areas of your brain are involved...

SCREECH!

WHICH BIT DEALS WITH HEADACHES?

THE PART OF THE CORTEX THAT DEALS WITH HEARING

SEPARATE AREAS ON THE RIGHT SIDE OF THE CORTEX THAT DEAL WITH MELODY AND PITCH

In the 1970s US neurophysiologists Joseph Bogen and Harold Gordon studied these areas. They injected a powerful painkiller into blood vessels that fed the right side of their patients' brains. This put the right side of the brains to sleep for a while. When the patients tried to sing using only the left sides of their brain what did they sound like?

a) They sang beautifully, like trained opera singers.
b) They could open their mouths but no sound came out.
c) They sounded like a calf bellowing.

ANSWER

c) Without the help of the right side of their cortex the singers couldn't produce a tune. Mind you, some people seem to have this problem with both sides of their brain in working order.

TEACHER'S TEA-BREAK TEASER
A note to the reader: You try this teaser at your own risk, OK? Don't blame me if you get expelled. To do it all you have to do is sing loudly outside the staff room...

Words are controlled by the left side of your brain and tunes by the right. When you sing it's hard for your cortex to cope with two sets of information at the same time. I mean – just think, you have to access your memory centres to remember what the words and notes actually sound like. Very musical people actually grow extra neurons in the areas of the right cortex that deal with sound and hearing. OK, got all that? No? Why not ask your brain to chew it over…

THINK FOR YOURSELF (IT'S NOT THAT EASY)

1 Thinking is the way that your brain makes sense of the world and organizes the information it gets from your senses. Scientists believe that thinking is a wave of brain activity that spreads as neurons fire signals at each other. Does that get you thinking?

2 The brain has different areas for different jobs like talking or sniffing things, remember. But neurons all over the cortex are involved in thinking and the active areas vary according to what you're doing. Your level of concentration or even your feelings can affect the pattern of brain activity.

3 Brain neurons fire most of the time, and scientists think that this could mean your brain is vaguely mulling over past memories. The increased activity caused by thinking might be due to your brain drawing on memories to build up a particular thought. **4** When you do two different things at once each half of your brain has separate thoughts. Is that a good thing? Well, maybe you're in two minds about it.

BET YOU NEVER KNEW!

There is no limit to the number of thoughts you can have. So you don't believe me? Well, read on. Your brain has billions of nerve cells, remember that bit? If you look at a neuron magnified 10,000 times it appears like a tiny tree with over 5,000 branches.

Scientists think there are more than 100,000,000,000,000 that's ONE HUNDRED TRILLION brain synapses. (These are the gaps between neurons, remember.) And scientists believe a thought can travel through these synapses in ANY order. So there may be more possible routes for a thought than atoms in the entire universe. And that means that there's NO LIMIT to the thinking power of your brain.

WOW! That really was something to think about. But oddly enough, although your brain is unbelievably powerful it finds doing several things at once a bit of a strain...

COULD YOU BE A SCIENTIST?

Some psychologists gave two students a brain-teasing task.

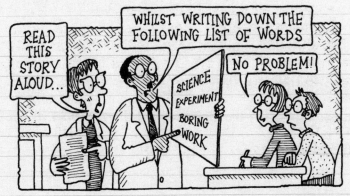

How do you think the students got on?

a) They were useless. The brain simply can't manage to read, talk, listen and write all at the same time.

b) The students found themselves writing the story and repeating out loud the lists the scientists were reading to them.

c) Although the students started off slowly and made mistakes they soon learnt how to do the tasks at the same time.

And speaking of talking or talking about speaking the next bit of this chapter will really get your tongue wagging.

SPEAK FOR YOURSELF

Try listening to yourself talking and you'll realize that speech is full of hesitation – er ... (sorry, bit of a hesitation there), repetition and mistakes. Yep – speaking is one of the hardest things your brain gets up to. In order to talk properly you've got to...

• Access your memory (**1**) for the correct words and your memory of how to pronounce them.

• Use the Broca's area (**2**) of your cortex to pronounce the words correctly. It should send a message to the bit of the cortex that controls the movement of your vocal cords, tongue and lips to speak the words. You will need your cerebellum (**3**) to co-ordinate all these complex movements.

• Use your Wernicke's area (**4**) to put the words in the right grammatical order. (See page 28 for info on how these areas were discovered.)

• You will need your ears and the part of the cortex that deals with listening (**5**) to hear your words and the rest of your cortex to check they make sense.

It's (not) that easy! Yet amazingly scientists have found that a good speaker can speak up to three words a second even when someone is mumbling in their ear.

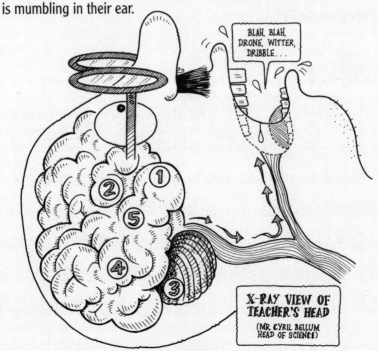

BLAH, BLAH, DRONE, WITTER, DRIBBLE...

X-RAY VIEW OF TEACHER'S HEAD

(MR. CYRIL BELLUM HEAD OF SCIENCE)

UNSPEAKABLE SPEECH PROBLEMS

But of course, things can go wrong. Usually at embarrassing moments like when you're talking to someone really famous and important. Sometimes you say the right words in the right order but because your cortex hasn't checked what you're saying the words sound really stupid. Here's US baseball commentator and manager Jerry Coleman:

"THE LATE START IS DUE TO THE TIME"

Spoonerisms are when you muddle up the first letters or sounds in a series of words.

Spoonerisms are named after British clergyman William Spooner (1844–1930) who was famous for them. He once told a student "you have hissed all my mystery lectures". Can you work out what old Spooner meant to say?

BET YOU NEVER KNEW!

1 About one in a hundred children suffer from stammering. Stammering is jerky, hesitant speech in which the first sounds of some words are often repeated. Sufferers report that they know what they want to say but they can't say it.

2 Scientists aren't quite sure what causes stammering but it seems to affect boys more than girls and it seems to be made worse by worry. It's probably linked to a problem in the Broca's area.

3 In the Middle Ages the problem was thought to be due to the tongue not working properly and useless cures were tried such as burning the tongue with a hot iron.

4 Nowadays stammering can be overcome by helping the sufferer to feel more relaxed when talking. Techniques used include learning to speak more slowly and to begin words with a more gentle movement of the lips and tongue.

READ ALL ABOUT IT

So how are you getting on reading this book? Finding it easy or having a bit of bother with some of the incomprehensible inapprehensible numinous words?

Go on, have a go at remembering them – they're numinous words for bamboozling science teachers.

Scientists reckon that children learn about ten new words a day at school – but that's not such a bad thing because everywhere you look there are written words.

A grown-up who reads a daily paper might get through about 100,000 words every week. This includes all the words they might read in an office job, road signs and even the back of cornflakes packets.

RIVETING READING

Reading is great. You can settle down with a good book and forget about the rest of the world. But you won't even reach the end of this sentence without the help of your brain. Here's your chance to discover what your brain is up to when you read. Simply listen in to some more of those fascinating Neuro-phone calls...

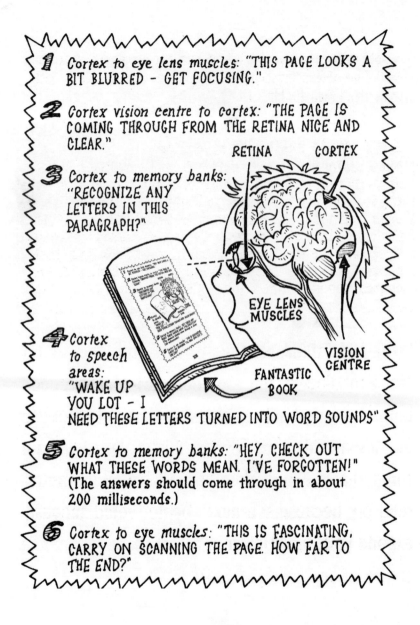

1 Cortex to eye lens muscles: "THIS PAGE LOOKS A BIT BLURRED – GET FOCUSING."

2 Cortex vision centre to cortex: "THE PAGE IS COMING THROUGH FROM THE RETINA NICE AND CLEAR."

3 Cortex to memory banks: "RECOGNIZE ANY LETTERS IN THIS PARAGRAPH?"

RETINA   CORTEX

EYE LENS MUSCLES

VISION CENTRE

FANTASTIC BOOK

4 Cortex to speech areas: "WAKE UP YOU LOT – I NEED THESE LETTERS TURNED INTO WORD SOUNDS"

5 Cortex to memory banks: "HEY, CHECK OUT WHAT THESE WORDS MEAN. I'VE FORGOTTEN!" (The answers should come through in about 200 milliseconds.)

6 Cortex to eye muscles: "THIS IS FASCINATING, CARRY ON SCANNING THE PAGE. HOW FAR TO THE END?"

A note to the reader: Now ask your brain to move your eyes to the next chunk of text. This should take 30 milliseconds. Hey! Come back you haven't read this bit…

BET YOU NEVER KNEW!

Even really smart kids suffer from a condition called dyslexia that makes it harder for them to learn to read. If you have the condition you might see the words as back to front or moving about, and find it hard to turn the words into sounds. Dyslexia can be caused by genes. These are chemical codes found in most body cells that control the way they develop. In the brain, genes control the way that neurons develop and wire up.

Teachers think reading is vital, but they don't mean reading for fun — oh no. Teachers expect you to read boring books so you can learn lots of facts. Sounds a real pain? OK, so maybe you could use some really expert scientific advice? Well, better read on, because the next chapter could seriously expand your brainpower…

LOATHSOME LEARNING

Do you find learning fun? Do you tumble out of bed shouting…

YIPPEE! IT'S SCHOOL TODAY. MORE LOVELY FACTS TO LEARN!

Or do you crawl out of bed thinking…

OH NO, NOT ANOTHER BORING DAY LEARNING STUPID OLD SCIENCE

Well, cheer up! Learning is one of the most vital tasks of your bulging brain and it CAN be fun – but only if you've got something interesting to learn.

Like now – so read on.

Bulging brains fact file

Name:	Learning
Basic facts:	Here's how you learn...
	1 Someone tells you something.
	2 You remember it.
	3 You use this information to help you in whatever work you are doing.
Disgusting details:	Some psychologists believe that learning gets harder over the age of 25. This could be because the memory starts to weaken. But other scientists claim that learning gets easier as you get older. So why don't they send grown-ups back to school?

A few facts to learn (and make sure you do)

1 You learn things all the time – not just in school. You learn whenever you notice anything new or try out a new skill.

2 Learning can be nice or nasty: Nice things to learn: chocolate ice-cream tastes yummy.

Nasty thing to learn: eat too much and you'll want to throw up.

3 Most people learn by trial and error. Remember learning to ride a bike. But once you've learnt something you can do it effortlessly and without thinking. Like riding that bike.

TEACHER'S TEA-BREAK TEASER
Put a fly in your teacher's morning cuppa with this tricky teaser. And remember, if your teacher doesn't believe you — this fact is TRUE. Tap gently on the staffroom door. When it opens, smile brightly and enquire...

IS IT TRUE THAT THERE WERE ONCE PLANS TO INTRODUCE MACHINES TO DO THE JOB OF TEACHERS?

SPLUTTER!

Yes, in the 1960s US psychologist Burrhus Skinner invented a teaching machine called a didak. The machine showed a sentence and you had to complete it. If you got the answer right you got a chance to answer harder questions. Oh goody!

THE GOOD NEWS: The machine never told you off.

THE BAD NEWS: It couldn't answer your questions and didn't know how to chat.

BET YOU NEVER KNEW!

It doesn't matter whether they have real teachers or machines to help them – some kids have trouble learning. There are loads of possible reasons for this. Sometimes the difficulties are caused by dyslexia or an eye problem so the child can't read easily. More often the child isn't interested in the lessons. Or perhaps the lessons require skills such as speaking or writing that the child isn't good at. Oddly enough one psychologist who studied how the brain learns suffered learning difficulties as a lad...

Hall of fame: John B. Watson (1878–1958)
Nationality: American

As a boy John B. Watson had a problem with learning. Maybe that's why he was forever getting into trouble, starting fights and terrorizing his home town in South Carolina, USA.

As he grew older John got mixed up in crime. But when he turned 16 he had a sudden change of heart and started to study really hard at home. He had to study really hard because he had decided to go to university and become a scientist.

At university John continued to find learning difficult. He couldn't understand his teachers and their boring lectures (sound familiar?).

But he did become fascinated by how rats learn things. Here's what Watson's notebook may have looked like...

The Great Rat Experiment

Today's the BIG day!!! I'm planning to find out if rats can learn from a nasty experience. I've been working hard all week building a three-metre-long alley for the tests - I call it the "rat-run".

Stage 1 ⟵ RAT-RUN   ME

Now to try it out. Will the rat do the obvious and go and grab the food? YES! YES! YES!

The rat runs down the rat-run and grabs the food. Atta boy! This proves that learning happens when you give a rat something new - like the food. This changes the rat's behaviour. Now to test my idea a bit further.

NEXT DAY Stage 2

I've blocked off the rat-run with a thick glass barrier. Will the rat still go down it? Here goes...

Yes - like a streak of lightning and bumped his little nosy on the barrier. Oh dear, poor old ratty. If I'm right the new information about the barrier will change the rat's behaviour - let me see... CRUNCH! FOOD

NEXT DAY **Stage three** ⋘ ⋘ ⋘ ⋘ ⋘

I've unblocked the rat-run. Will the rat still run? Maybe he's learnt that he'll get hurt. So he won't take the risk. Yep, he's scared - he's actually turning up his sore little schnozzle at the chance of that lovely food. **NO THANKS!**

Well, that proves my point. Rats can change the way they act by learning from a bad experience.

Hmm - I reckon it's just the same for humans, like me. My old teacher certainly taught me a few nasty lessons. I learnt I'd get a beating if I bunked off school.

Watson's experiments inspired a whole new movement of psychologists called behaviourists who believed that you could help rats – or humans – learn with rewards or punishments. But although Watson was certain that you could learn about human behaviour from studying rats there were squeaks of protest from other scientists when he compared humans to rats…

Eventually Watson resigned his university job to go into advertising. Here he put his ideas on learning into practice by selling baby powder. Watson reckoned:

1 Rats chased down the rat-run because they learnt there was food at the end. So by giving the rats a reward you could change their behaviour.

2 You could use advertising to give people the impression that by buying your brand of baby powder they would feel happier and be better parents. This feeling would be a kind of reward. So people would choose to buy your brand.

But did the plan work? What do you think?

a) Watson was sacked after featuring a rat on the advertising posters.

b) Watson's plan failed. People can't be compared to rats. We don't have to feel good when we go shopping.

c) Watson's plan worked and he became a millionaire. His ideas form the basis of modern advertising.

ANSWER

c) If advertising teaches you that buying a product will improve your life, then you'll probably feel like buying it.

I LOVE MEN WHO SMELL OF PONGY

ARE YOU INTELLIGENT?

Are you good at learning things? If so, you may be intelligent. But you might be surprised to know that psychologists don't agree what intelligence is all about. Many, though, believe that intelligence means an ability to solve new problems. Anyway, whatever you call it – intelligence, being clever, smart or brainy – here's a quick intelligence test to put you through your paces.

TRUE OR FALSE?
1 People with small heads aren't as intelligent as people with big heads. This is because people with big heads have bigger brains. TRUE/FALSE

BRAINY

NOT BRAINY

2 As you learn new skills your genes help you develop new neuron connections and links in your cortex so that you can remember them. TRUE/FALSE

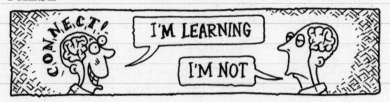

3 Playing lots of computer games can make you more intelligent. TRUE/FALSE

4 Eating fish is good for your brain. TRUE/FALSE

1 FALSE. Your brain size is nothing to do with intelligence. For example at 8 kg an elephant's brain is more than five times heavier than ours, but no one fancies an elephant to win this year's Nobel Prize. **2** TRUE. Your genes are constantly influencing the way your neurons re-wire themselves and all that depends on what skills you choose to learn and practise. So go ahead – learn how to read Russian and sing opera whilst juggling on a unicycle – your brilliant brain will re-wire itself for the job! **3** FALSE. But scientists think that children who play lots of computer games develop extra connections in the area of the cortex that controls delicate hand movements. This helps them play the games faster and win more often. **4** TRUE – maybe. Munching fish fingers for tea won't turn you into Einstein but fish contains brain goodies. There's iodine to speed up the way that your cells (including neurons) work, amino acids to make neuron chemicals such as noradrenaline and fatty acids that help your neurons repair themselves.

BULGING BRAIN DEVELOPMENT

Did you know that you learnt half of everything you know in your first five years?

YOU MEAN IT'S TAKEN YOU 75 YEARS TO LEARN THE OTHER HALF, GREAT-GRAN?

In some countries that's before children even start school! Oh, so you don't remember this vital learning period? Well, here's a quick reminder...

The first five years...

0 to six months

When you were born you could breathe, suck, swallow and then throw up, dribble, cry, sneeze, cough and stretch. And that's about all because your brain wasn't developed.

DRIBBLE! CRY! ATCHOO! COUGH! STRETCH! THAT'S BETTER

Six months

Your brain had doubled in size. The neurons were growing and branching and forming millions of synapses. You could roll over and smile. You could also copy the expressions on grown-up faces. (Don't try this now - you'll only get told off.)

One year

You had learnt how to pick things up with your hands and you had just spoken your first word. Before then grown-ups probably spoke to you in baby talk and you tried to make the same sounds back. But you hadn't got the hang of the tongue and lip movements so it came out as baby noises. You were just beginning to learn to walk, and falling over quite a lot.

I HATE RUSKS

GOO, GOO GAGA

Two years ...

You could walk run and speak about 274 words. Two vital words you learnt were "wee" and "poo". You were able to recognize the feeling when you had to go and now you could even tell people about it. Soon afterwards you learnt how to use a potty without making an embarrassing mess. And if things went wrong you could take off your underwear without help.

WEEEEE!

Three years

You could speak up to a 1,000 words in short sentences and feed yourself (but not at the same time). You were also learning to draw. Sometimes you were so wrapped up in your drawing or games you might poo or wee in your underwear.
(Hopefully this no longer happens.)

PONG

Four years

WELL DONE!

Your brain was four times bigger than when you were born. You were asking loads of questions using about 1,500 words, and going to the toilet all by yourself.

Five years

ARGH! SCHOOL!

You could tell stories and hop and skip and you knew about 2,000 words. And round about this time you started school.

The next few years...

After you turned six, things in your brain got a bit less hectic but the neuron links in your cortex carried on forming. Some time between the ages of six and ten most children learn the following skills:

Tick here

☐ How to play ball games really well.

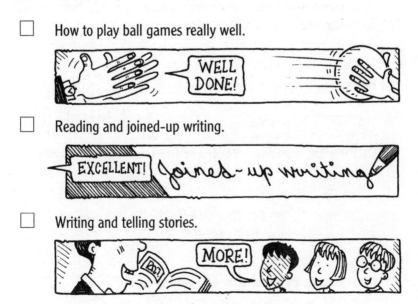

WELL DONE!

☐ Reading and joined-up writing.

EXCELLENT! Joined-up writing

☐ Writing and telling stories.

MORE!

☐ Drawing, painting and making models.

☐ Simple cooking and cleaning and even washing up. Oh yes – this is part of growing up, I'm afraid.

☐ Loads of facts and new words at school.

So how far have you got?

Of course not all kids develop at the same speed. Some are late-developers. That doesn't make them stupid – scientific mega-genius Albert Einstein didn't learn to talk until he was four. And girls' and boys' brains develop to different timetables anyway. For example, for reasons scientists can't quite explain, the parts of the cortex that deal with speech develop earlier in girls than boys. So girls often learn to talk earlier. And boys' and girls' brains go on developing in different ways at different times.

BOYS V GIRLS

Not surprisingly psychologists have found that boys and girls are better at different things...

BET YOU NEVER KNEW!

For example, girls may be better at talking than boys. Oh so you knew this already? Brain scans performed at Yale University School of Medicine, USA, show that men only use the left side of their brains to talk but women use both sides. But who comes out top overall – the battling boys or the gutsy girls?

Read on and
find out in...

THE BATTLE OF THE SEXES

Scientists have found that boys and girls tend to be better at different things. Of course, you might be different and scientists always argue about the results…

1 One study showed that boys are often quicker at solving tricky maths problems in their heads. Very gifted boys use the right sides of their brains to concentrate on the problem. But girls tend to use both sides and waste time putting their thoughts into words.

2 When boys and girls are given 3-D puzzles to assemble, the boys are better at imagining what the finished puzzle will look like. Once again girls tend to waste time explaining to themselves in words how they will solve the puzzle.

3 But girls' brains are better at controlling their finger movements for delicate fiddly tasks. So the girls might well be quicker at putting the puzzle together.

4 Boys tend to have a good sense of direction. They are very good at building up a clear idea of a route in the right side of their brains.

5 But they're not so good at remembering landmarks. Girls with their better memory for words can remember the landmarks even if they're sometimes less sure about the direction.

Important note: In conclusion, every scientific study has found that boys and girls have differing abilities in some areas and use their brains in different ways. But, and here's the important bit, OVERALL, THEY ARE EQUALLY CLEVER. So shut it, OK?

And there you have it. Learning is a vital function of your bulging brain. Now, have you learnt everything in this chapter? Well, one thing's for certain – you won't have learnt anything without a memory. Luckily, the next mind-expanding chapter can help you. And you'll soon find those memories flooding back...

MIXED-UP MEMORY

Welcome to this unforgettable chapter. It's about memory. Just what is this mysterious ability? And how does it work? And will you remember anything after you've read this book? Er ... now what was I talking about?

Bulging brains fact file

Name: Memory

Basic facts: Memory works like this...

1 You sense something.

2 You put it in your memory.

3 You can recall the memory when something reminds you of it. The reminder might be a word, an event or even a smell.

Disgusting details:

...BUT I JUST TOLD YOU ABOUT SHORT TERM MEMORY!

THAT WAS 40 SECONDS AGO, MISS

...OF COURSE CHALKY ONLY TOOK ONE SUGAR IN HIS TEA – IT WAS HARD STUFF TO GET HOLD OF SEVENTY YEARS AGO

You've got not one but three memories.

1 Short-term memory. Useful for phone numbers, etc. You forget these memories in 30 seconds. Some kids store their science knowledge in here.

2 Long-term memory. This is stuff you remember for years. It's where Grandpa stores all those boring old yarns of life when he was a lad. These first two memory systems are based in your cortex.

3 A special memory for skills like riding a bike that you can use without being aware of having to remember them. This memory seems to be based in your cerebellum.

MYSTERIOUS LONG-TERM MEMORY-MAKER

Stuck in the limbic system of your brain is an interesting brain bit called the hippocampus (hippo-camp-us). According to scientists your helpful hippocampus helps to turn your short-term recollections into linked-up neurons. And they form memories that you can remember for the rest of your life. In 1953 an American who suffered from fits had his hippocampus taken out. The fits stopped but the poor man lost his ability to remember things. He still had his memories of life before the op, though.

Hopefully your memory is much better? Well, let's pick up the Neuro-phone and check out how it works…

A MEMORABLE JOKE

The brain is about to try and remember a joke…

(OK, I didn't say the joke was any good.)

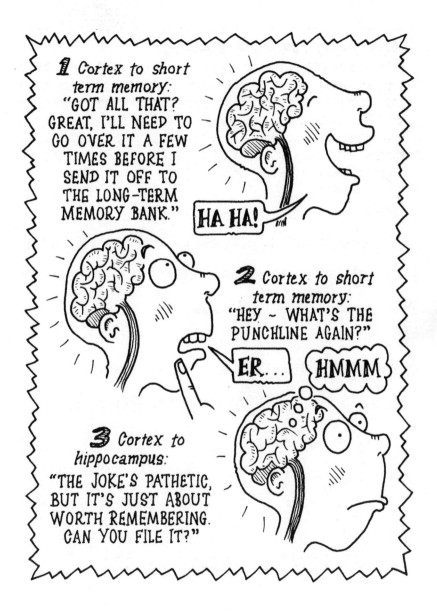

Scientific note

So how does it happen? Scientists reckon that the neurons produce chemicals called proteins that make it easier to send a message across certain synapses. This creates pathways through the neuron maze in your bulging brain. (It's thought that each pathway is storing a part of the memory. Some store colours and others can store shapes.) The memory of the joke should remain in your brain even if you can't recall it. People call this "sub-conscious memory".

A few weeks later...

4 Cortex to memory banks: "GOT THAT JOKE ABOUT THE DOG FILED? I WAS JUST WONDERING WHERE I HEARD IT."

5 Memory banks: "YEAH, IT'S HERE. I'LL JUST CHECK ITS SOURCE... DON'T YOU REMEMBER, IT WAS IN THAT *BULGING BRAINS* BOOK."

6 Cortex: "BLIMEY, SO IT WAS!"

No doubt you'll be pleased to hear there's room in your memory for lots more jokes (and other stuff). Remember all those billions of neurons and synapses in your cortex? Well, scientists reckon you can squeeze facts in your memory to fill 20,000 encyclopaedias. Do that and your brain really would be bulging. You might even win a memory competition…

THE HORRIBLE SCIENCE MEMORY COMPETITION

This competition is unforgettable. All the prize winners have shown powers of recollection that will live long in our memories.

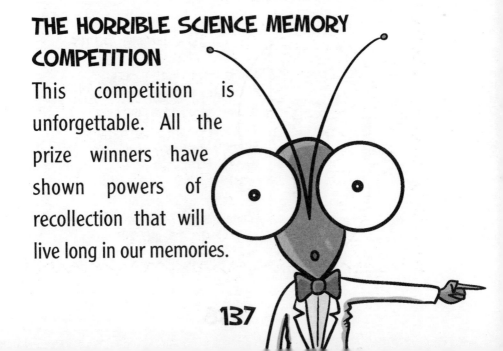

137

Fourth Prize

German conductor Hans von Bülow (1830–1894)

Hans was never one to forget a good tune. One day he took the train from Hamburg to Berlin and read the music of a new symphony. That evening he conducted the entire symphony without any mistakes *entirely from memory.*

ERRR – OH YES, I REMEMBER TUM-TE-TUM...

FLUSH!

56937 09785

Third Prize

You'd think that remembering boring numbers would be hard. But in 1995 **Hiroyuki Goto of Japan** recited the mathematical number pi to 42,195 places with no mistakes. The performance took over 17 hours including breaks to go to the toilet. At the end I expect he was flushed with success.

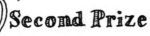

Second Prize

Devout **Mehmed Ali Halici of Turkey**
recited 6,666 verses of religious text

BLAH BLAH

AND NOW FOR VERSE 3772...

in 1967. Could you do that in your school assembly? Come to think of it would you fancy an assembly that was 18 hours long?

First Prize

I WILL NOW RECITE THE ENTIRE BIBLE... IN LATIN

Goes to **Russian Solomon Veniaminoff.** Solomon wanted to be a violinist but an ear disease slightly damaged his hearing. In the 1930s he decided to become a journalist. Later he worked as a stage entertainer where he wowed the crowds with his unforgettable talent for remembering incredibly long numbers or lists of words. From time to time he also helped psychologist Alexander Luria (1902–1977) with his work on memory. Here's Solomon's story. Of course, we can't remember the exact details but this story is based on the real facts...

THE MAN WHO NEVER FORGOT

Moscow, May 1928

The slender young man was clearly on edge. "My name is Solomon," he stammered. "My editor sent me to see you because of my memory."

"What's wrong with it?" asked Alexander Luria curiously as he leaned back in his rocking-chair. Solomon nervously swept his black hair from his eyes.

"People say that I have an exceptional memory. The fact is I can remember every single thing that has happened to me since I was one year old."

"Fascinating but unlikely," smiled Luria. There was an uncomfortable silence broken only by the ticking of the large old clock on the mantelpiece. Then Luria sighed.

"Oh well, I suppose we'd better test you. I'd like you to try to remember this sequence of numbers."

The scientist quickly jotted down a series of 30 numbers and then read them out to the young man.

Solomon looked even more worried and gazed briefly into nothing. His dark, dreamy eyes seemed fixed on a distant object that Luria couldn't see.

Then he repeated the numbers perfectly.

The scientist's mouth dropped open. "But that's astounding!" he gasped.

"I could say them backwards if you like," said Solomon quietly. And he gave a shy, fleeting smile.

1958

Thirty years later Alexander Luria sat in the warm sunshine gazing vacantly at his garden. He was lost in thought and as usual he felt rather tired. In front of him lay a pile of old papers covered in his spidery handwriting. The paper was crinkled and yellow with age.

"So how do I turn all this into a book?" he mused to himself. "Where to begin, that's the first problem."

"Why not begin at the beginning?" said a voice. Luria looked up in surprise at the man sitting quietly in the corner. The visitor's hair was grey with age and his figure was stooped and thick-set.

"Oh, Solomon I'm so sorry, I quite forgot you were here. Now what were we saying?"

"We were discussing the book you were going to write about memory and our 30 years of working together. That's why you invited me here at 4.24 p.m. yesterday."

"Has it really been that long?" asked the scientist wearily.

"Well, on and off, when I wasn't working on the stage."

"I think I'll begin my book on that day in June, when was it? 1929 when you first came to see me."

"It was 1928," said Solomon firmly, "and the month was May. I remember you in your grey suit sitting in your rocking-chair. And that old-fashioned clock you had. And then those 30 numbers ... what were they now? 62, 30, 19, 41..."

Luria gazed in growing shock at the first page of his yellowing notes. Yes, there in his own handwriting was the exact sequence of numbers repeated with eerie accuracy over a gap of 30 years.

"But that's astounding!" he wheezed breathlessly.

"That's what you said at the time," said Solomon with his familiar shy smile.

"But you must have remembered millions of pieces of information since then. You're a lucky man Solomon, I do admire this gift of yours."

"It's no gift!" exclaimed Solomon bitterly. "As I told you in 1928 it's a curse. I often wished I could forget things. Sometimes all these facts and numbers and lists jostle in my mind like a huge crowd – like words in poetry or sparks in a fireworks display. They drive me crazy! The greatest gift is to forget things. But that's one gift I will never possess. Forgetting is a wonderful thing."

And his eyes sparkled with tears.

SOLOMON'S SECRET

After years of patient study Luria figured out the secret of Solomon Veniaminoff's astonishing memory. It was due to the way his mind worked. Solomon suffered from a disease called synaesthesia (sin-ees-thees-ia). Incredible though it sounds this rare brain disease made Solomon experience sounds as colours. He told one psychologist:

By remembering the colours he saw when hearing things and by imagining numbers as people he found it easy to remember tons of information. But the only way he could ever forget something was to imagine it was written on paper and he was burning it.

BOOST YOUR MEMORY

Would you want a memory like Solomon's? Probably not – but with a more powerful memory you could get top marks in your science tests every time and even remember your dad's birthday. The good news is you don't need a special brain to develop an excellent memory.

PICTURE THIS...

But don't worry, there are many less painful methods of improving your memory. Here's one of them. Supposing tomorrow you have a science test and you need to remember to feed the goldfish and take your sandwiches to school.

1 *Try* to remember to do these things. This should store the information in your short-term memory.

2 For reasons that scientists don't quite understand you can remember pictures better than facts. It might be because you can link pictures with other memories more easily and in some way this makes them easier to recall. So make up a mental picture to help you remember. For example, you could imagine your teacher eating a goldfish in a sandwich.

3 When you get up the next morning and get ready for school, the thought of facing your teacher again will immediately make you remember the image of her eating a goldfish sandwich. So you use your teacher as a memory cue – that's a kind of clue to help you remember the goldfish, the sandwiches and the test, stupid.

TERROR IN THE AIR

Your memory can be affected by your feelings. In the 1950s Mitchell Berkun, a scientist working for the US Army, dreamt up this horrible experiment.

1 Take a group of army recruits up in a plane.

2 Right, you guys. Here's the emergency drill. Make sure you listen good and proper. There's 12 steps to remember. Your life may depend on getting them right.

3 ...and finally item 12. You inflate your life-jacket by pulling the cord. Got all that?

Er, I think so.

4 What are those fire engines doing on the ground?

Of course, the whole incident including the fire engines on the ground had been set up by Berkun. The terrible test showed that the recruits could only remember half the instructions when they were scared out of their wits.

And talking about feelings … the next chapter's all about them – the highs, the lows, the excitement and the horror. So, do you feel like reading a bit further?

FORCEFUL FEELINGS

A re you a touchy-feely person who is always laughing or weeping? Do you pride yourself on being the strong, silent type? Well, whatever you're like on the surface, your brain is bulging with powerful feelings.

FEELING THE FORCE

Scientists claim there are six types of emotion that people feel all over the world. Huh – what do they know? When was the last time you saw an emotional scientist? Well, we've managed to find one and photograph the full range of his six emotions.

Of course, feelings can get horribly mixed up. That's why people cry when they're happy or sometimes feel a bit down after some good news.

Scientists have scarcely begun to explain why our emotions get so tangled. However, as you're about to discover, emotions can be triggered by several different chemicals. With so many of these chemicals sloshing about at the same time it wouldn't be surprising if your brain got some mixed messages.

COMPLICATED FEELINGS

Feeling emotion is actually more complicated than you might think. For one thing you need to co-ordinate three areas of your brain. And that really gets the Neuro-phone lines buzzing. Just listen to this: Your teacher is telling you off...

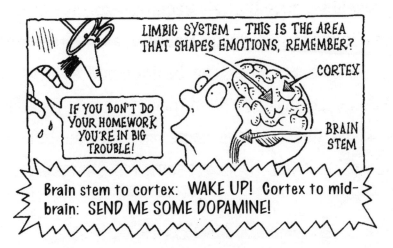

Brain stem to cortex: WAKE UP! Cortex to mid-brain: SEND ME SOME DOPAMINE!

Dopamine (dope-a-mean) is a chemical that seems to make your neurons more active and fire more signals. Obviously the emotion you feel depends on what's going on. It could be terror or joy or anything in between.

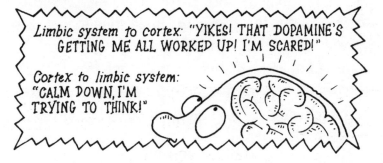

Limbic system to cortex: "YIKES! THAT DOPAMINE'S GETTING ME ALL WORKED UP! I'M SCARED!"

Cortex to limbic system: "CALM DOWN, I'M TRYING TO THINK!"

BULGING BRAIN EXPRESSIONS

One neurologist says to another...

IS YOUR WORK INTERESTING?

WELL MY **RAS** IS FIRED UP!

Is that some kind of stove?

ANSWER

No. The reticular (ret-tick-u-lar) activating system or RAS for short is the area in the brain stem that makes you conscious and alert. By the way, you might be interested to know that in small kids the RAS is easily switched on and that's why they get so easily scared. As you grow up the RAS quietens down because your cortex learns when there's a real monster and when it's just a curtain blowing in a darkened room.

DIZZY DOPAMINE V SERIOUS SEROTONIN

So dopamine shakes up your limbic system and you feel emotion. But you don't always do what you feel like doing. That's because of another brain chemical called serotonin (seer-ro-tone-in). This is squirted by neurons linking the limbic system and the cortex. Serotonin tends to calm the neurons down and makes you feel more sensible. (It can also make you feel happy and relaxed.)

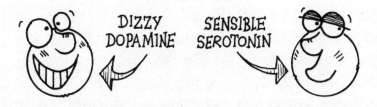

DIZZY DOPAMINE   SENSIBLE SEROTONIN

Imagine you've guzzled some lovely cream buns and you're greedily eyeing up the rest.

 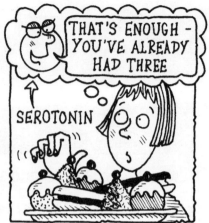

In other words serotonin tells you *not* to do things. It's like having a sensible teacher stuck between your ears. (Now that *is* a scary thought!)

By now you might be wondering why your cortex needs to get involved in feelings. After all, you feel things in the limbic system and you've got dizzy dopamine to get you all worked up and serious serotonin to calm you down. Well, the cortex is there to think things over and make the ultimate decision...

NO THANK, YOU, ANOTHER BUN MIGHT MAKE ME FEEL SICK

And of course, getting your cortex involved helps you stop to think when you get emotional. This can help you control your temper.

BET YOU NEVER KNEW!

Scientists believe that people with low levels of serotonin can become bad-tempered or even violent. That's because they find it harder to control their feelings. And talking about uncontrollable feelings...

HORRIBLE SCIENCE
HEALTH WARNING

There's a feeling of TERROR lurking just over the page.

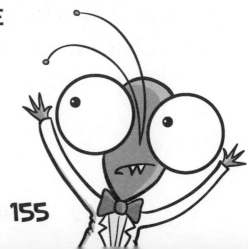

FEAR AND FURY

Although feelings are controlled and felt in your brain, your body also joins in and helps you to feel emotions. Sometimes in a horrible way. Just imagine you haven't done your homework for the third time running: your teacher is seething. Never mind, here's your chance to make interesting scientific observations on the effect of anger and fear…

An angry teacher

ADRENAL GLANDS OVER KIDNEYS SQUIRTING A HORMONE CALLED ADRENALINE (AD-REN-A-LIN) INTO THE BLOOD. THIS CAUSES ALL THE OTHER EFFECTS...

WILKINS, I WANT A WORD WITH YOU...

Stored sugar pouring out of liver into blood and on its way to feed the raging brain

Lungs panting in air – ten times more than usual

Adrenal glands

Digestion stopped

Fat being dissolved and sent to the muscles to provide energy for violent physical action. (This might sound a bit extreme for a teacher but remember those bodily reactions developed millions of years ago to help early people fight woolly mammoths and other fierce creatures.)

Did someone mention scientific observations? Well, maybe you're not in the mood. Inside you might be feeling a bit wobbly, petrified even. Maybe a bit like this...

A scared child

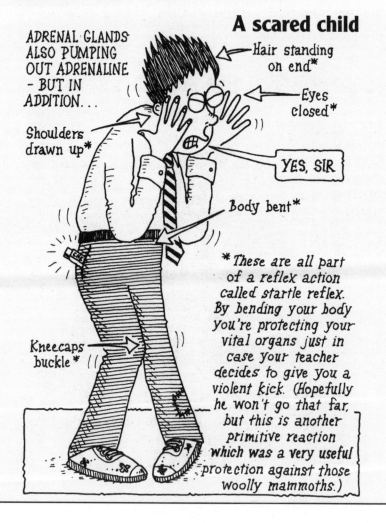

ADRENAL GLANDS ALSO PUMPING OUT ADRENALINE - BUT IN ADDITION...

Hair standing on end*

Eyes closed*

Shoulders drawn up*

YES, SIR

Body bent*

Kneecaps buckle*

*These are all part of a reflex action called startle reflex. By bending your body you're protecting your vital organs just in case your teacher decides to give you a violent kick. (Hopefully he won't go that far, but this is another primitive reaction which was a very useful protection against those woolly mammoths.)

Important note:

Oh no! Your teacher's figured out it was you who absent-mindedly left chewing gum on his chair. Oh-er, you're going to cop it now. TAKE COVER! YOUR TEACHER IS ABOUT TO GO BALLISTIC…

A teacher who is just about to explode

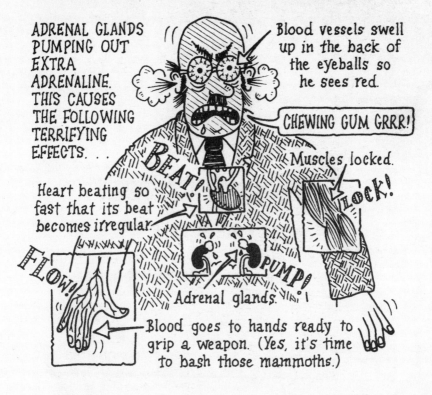

ADRENAL GLANDS PUMPING OUT EXTRA ADRENALINE. THIS CAUSES THE FOLLOWING TERRIFYING EFFECTS…

Blood vessels swell up in the back of the eyeballs so he sees red.

CHEWING GUM GRRR!

Muscles locked.

LOCK!

BEAT!

Heart beating so fast that its beat becomes irregular.

PUMP!

Adrenal glands.

FLOW!

Blood goes to hands ready to grip a weapon. (Yes, it's time to bash those mammoths.)

An even more scared child

White face. (Blood drains out of the skin so that any wounds you get won't bleed too much. Another sensible Stone Age precaution.)

Spit dries up. GULP!

JIBBER TREMBLE!

THUMP! THUMP!

Heart speeds up.

The long, long, long wait outside the head teacher's room

So you've been sent for a little chat with the head teacher? Oh dear, this could prove painful. Here are a few things to think about whilst you're waiting for the axe to fall...

FOUR FEARFUL FEELINGS FACTS

1 You feel stress. This is the fear you feel when you're scared but you can't run away. Well, you can but they'll only catch you and then you'll really catch it. Some kids feel stress when they start a new school and some feel it every day they go to school.

2 Chewing your fingernails yet? Masticating keratin* is a common response to stress.

Scientists think that people feel more cheerful when they chew things. It's healthier to chew gum (sugar-free, of course) but that's what got you into this mess. By the way, when you're stressed out your sense of taste stops working. So the gum would taste like someone's already chewed it.

3 Your adrenal glands are squirting a hormone called cortisone (cor-ti-zone). The aim of this

*(Mas-tic-kate-ing) = posh term for chewing. (Ker-rat-in) = the substance your nails are made of.

chemical is to prepare your muscles for action later on. Sugar pours into your blood, your brain feels more alert because it's getting more sugar and the nerves are firing like crazy. But you feel rotten – all nervy and jittery. Yikes!

4 You'd better apologize to the head teacher – you might even be let off without a punishment. But there's one feeling that's even worse than being stressed. It's worse because it makes you feel really miserable, really sad. It can spoil your whole life…

BET YOU NEVER KNEW!

Depression is a brain condition that makes you so miserable you want to go to bed and cry and stay there for ever. Scientists think it may be the result of a shortage of brain chemicals such as serotonin. If you ever feel this way try taking a deep breath. Let it out slowly and relax. Yep, that's it: for some reason relaxing actually helps you feel better. Remember this rotten scary fearful miserable feeling is caused by a few chemicals in your bulging brain.

THE SECRET OF HAPPINESS

For hundreds of years people have searched for this elusive secret and got very uptight and miserable because they couldn't find it. But it's here, here in this very book! In the 1970s two US psychologists tried to find out what makes a happy or sad personality. They discovered that: it helps if you enjoy meeting new people...

It's best not to expect too much from life. That way good things come as a pleasant surprise.

But always look for the bright side of every situation.

OH GOOD!
I *LOVE*
SWIMMING

And if you can't find happiness by using these simple techniques then don't worry. Science has found ways of making you cheer up whether you like it or not...

BET YOU NEVER KNEW!

1 In the 1950s it was common to treat diseases of the mind by cutting the nerves to the front part of the cortex. This made the patient less emotional (maybe that's because it's hard to be emotional when you've got a thumping headache).

2 US surgeon Walter Freeman invented his own version of this horrible treatment. Walt stuck an ice-pick through a patient's eye-socket into the brain and cut the nerves that way. I expect he only wanted to pick their brains, ha-ha. Hardened doctors were known to swoon at this revolting spectacle. The patients also felt sick and confused afterwards.

3 In 1963 scientist RG Heath tried a new technique to control feelings. He stuck electrodes in the brain of a man with a brain disease that caused uncontrollable rages. By pressing buttons the man gave electric shocks to different areas of his brain. When he shocked areas such as the tegmentum (teg-men-tum), a region of the mid-brain under the cortex, the man felt rather more cheerful.

But you don't have to drill holes in your skull or wield ice-picks or even suffer electric shocks to feel emotional. Try tuning into your favourite music. Yep, why not enjoy the feel-good factor with our exclusive relaxation music…?

The Horrible Science
♪ *Feelgood Music* ♪

Recorded by Austrian psychologist Manfred Clynes...

Sponsored by Soothie-Bonce Headache Tablets.

BEFORE   AFTER

Chill out to the brain calming tones of musical gems such as "The Brandenberg Concertos" by German composer JS Bach (1685-1750)

IMPORTANT NOTE:

Yeah, it's dead boring classical stuff by an even more dead composer. But *Clynes* found that people all over the world go gooey when they listen to it. Yes, even people like you who think classical music is best enjoyed by zombies and elderly teachers. So get in the groove, chill out and feel mellow...

COULD YOU BE A SCIENTIST?

The situation you're in and the reactions of other people can affect the way you feel. Sounds like common sense, doesn't it? But psychologists have tried to find out precisely how important these factors are. And they've dreamt up a few brain-boggling experiments…

1 In the late 1960s two psychologists from New York University, USA, played frisbee in the waiting-room of Grand Central station. They laughed and joked and got in the way. After a while they threw the frisbee to a third scientist who was pretending to be a stranger. She joined in the game. What happened next?

a) Other people joined in the game.
b) Everyone ignored the frisbee players.
c) The scientists were arrested for causing a nuisance.

2 The same team put three people in a room and gave them forms to fill in. Then they wafted smoke through vents to make it look like the room was on fire. Two of the people were actually psychologists in disguise and they ignored the smoke. What did the third person do?

a) Ran about shouting...

b) Ignored the smoke.

c) Got a fire extinguisher and squirted the scientists with foam from head to foot.

3 US psychologist Philip Zimbardo set up a tasteless experiment. A nice, friendly scientist was given the job of persuading complete strangers to eat fried grasshoppers. Next, another scientist rudely ordered people to eat the insects.

What did the results show?
a) People were more likely to eat the grasshoppers when they were asked nicely.
b) The test was scrapped when someone threw up. This is odd because grasshoppers are a delicacy in parts of Africa such as Morocco. They have a lovely crunchy texture and taste like dried shrimp.
c) People ate the grasshoppers on both occasions. But they said they felt different when they were ordered to eat them.

FANCY A NIBBLE?

SIZZLE!

ANSWERS

All the experiments show how your view of the situation can shape your feelings.

1 a) When one person joined the game everyone else felt good enough to want to take part. The scientists actually had trouble halting it. In another experiment the "stranger" pretended to be grumpy and no one else got involved.

2 b) If everyone else ignores an event – even a dangerous fire – it's hard to feel excited about it.

3 c) When people were asked nicely, they said they ate the grasshoppers because they didn't want to upset the nice scientist. When the people were ordered to eat, they said they felt like trying the grasshoppers anyway.

Mind you, there's one situation where you'd feel nothing. It's when you get knocked out cold by a bash on the head. And if you want to find out what it does to your brain take a look at the next chapter. It's a real knockout.

BANGS 'N' BASHES

As you've probably realized by now, the brain is an intricate and delicate bit of equipment. So, not surprisingly, a bash on the head can damage the brain in all sorts of horrible and unexpected ways. Luckily, you do have a bit of natural protection.

BULGING BRAIN PROTECTION

Your bulging brain is naturally well protected. Let's take a look at this MRI scan.

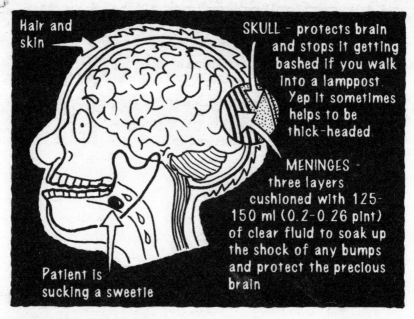

Hair and skin

SKULL – protects brain and stops it getting bashed if you walk into a lamppost. Yep it sometimes helps to be thick-headed.

MENINGES – three layers cushioned with 125-150 ml (0.2-0.26 pint) of clear fluid to soak up the shock of any bumps and protect the precious brain

Patient is sucking a sweetie

A NASTY BLOW

Despite these elaborate defences a bash on the bonce can make you lose your memory – or cause amnesia to use the scientific term. In this state you can't remember what hit you, or even that you've been hit. And you may lose consciousness. And consciousness is actually the most incredible thing your bulging brain gets up to…

Bulging brains fact file

Name:	Consciousness
Basic facts:	It means being aware of your thoughts and feelings. Scientists aren't too sure how this happens. The whole of your cortex seems to be involved in making you aware of your thoughts and what they mean.
Disgusting details:	It's possible to run around and perform simple actions whilst unconscious. In the 1956 FA Cup Final, goalkeeper Bert Trautmann was knocked unconscious in a collision with an opposing player. But battling Bert somehow made a vital save and completed the game. His team, Manchester City, won the cup.

BULGING BRAIN BUMPS

Here are some vital facts to bump up your knowledge.

1 When you get up in the morning your brain gets a rude awakening. As you lift your head up your brain slops forward and bangs against the front part of your skull.

Luckily your meninges and the fluid around the brain stop it getting too battered.

2 Some neurologists think the shock makes some people feel bad-tempered in the morning. (It's either that or the sour milk in their tea.)

3 In car crashes the effect of the brain being thrown forwards is far more damaging than a blow on the head. The shock is more likely to tear blood vessels and the brain itself, leaving wounds that cannot easily be treated because they're inside the skull.

4 The effects of an injury can depend on which part of the cortex gets damaged. It can lead to problems reading, smelling or tasting, or amnesia – that's loss of memory, remember?

5 In 1997 Vicky, a ten-year-old British girl, banged her head and started writing backwards and upside down. Vicky could read her own writing but it must have baffled her teacher. A year later she got overexcited watching football and banged her head again. The next day, for reasons that neurologists can't explain, her writing had returned to normal.

BET YOU NEVER KNEW!

In 1998 a retired Scottish footballer said that his memory loss was due to heading the ball too much. His wife said that he often chatted to his grandchildren and then forgot whom he was talking to. Before the 1950s, footballs were made of heavy leather and when it rained they sucked in water and got heavier. If they hit you on the head they could knock you out.

HORRIBLE HEALTH WARNING!

So let that be a warning. Don't go bashing your head against hard solid objects such as brick walls, floors or teachers. It's horribly unhealthy.

THUD!

BRICK WALL: HARD SOLID OBJECT

HEAD: NOT SUCH A HARD SOLID OBJECT

Bulging brains fact file

Name: Headache

Basic facts: A headache is a brain-pain. But wait a minute – didn't someone say the brain can't feel pain? This is true, but when you're under stress more blood squirts into your brain.

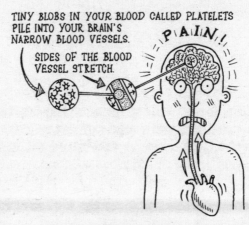

TINY BLOBS IN YOUR BLOOD CALLED PLATELETS PILE INTO YOUR BRAIN'S NARROW BLOOD VESSELS.

SIDES OF THE BLOOD VESSEL STRETCH.

PAIN!

Disgusting details:

ICE CREAM

A headache can be caused by eating ice cream. If the ice cream touches the roof of your mouth it shocks the nerves that lead to your brain. The best thing to do is to touch the roof of your mouth with your nice warm tongue. This relaxes the nerves. Alternatively, you could let the ice cream melt a bit before stuffing your little face.

TEACHER'S TEA-BREAK TEASER

All you do is choose a morning when your teacher has been teaching an extra-difficult class. He'll probably have a headache and will be gulping down a few painkillers with his tea. Tap quietly on the staffroom door (remember teachers have feelings too). When the door opens your teacher will be looking grim. So smile sweetly and enquire...

DOES FROWNING MAKE YOUR HEADACHE WORSE?

ANSWER

Frowning squishes the platelets in your teacher's blood vessels and makes the pain worse. Your teacher should smile to relax his blood vessels. Or take a painkiller. Some painkillers, such as paracetamol, stop the brain sensing pain so much, whilst others such as as ibuprofen tackle the swelling and other chemical changes in the aching area.

HORRIBLE HEADACHE CURES

And that's a lot better than the ancient Roman treatment for a headache. Roman doctor Scribonius Largus recommended whacking the patient on the head with an electric fish. This fishy shock treatment was supposed to cure the ache. It didn't. Mind you, if you lived in the Stone Age there weren't any of those nice painkillers or even an electric fish around.

STONE AGE BRAIN SURGERY

1 Take a sharp bit of flint.

2 Scrape the hair and skin off the patient's head.

3 Ignore any screams from the victim, sorry patient.

4 Carry on until a hole appears in the skull.

No one is sure why this operation was carried out in the Stone Age but it was used in ancient Greece to tackle persistent headaches. Although it didn't do much good the victims often survived with their brains bulging out of the gory hole. Stone Age skulls have been found in which the skull had started to heal.

Actually this treatment – known today as trepanning – is still performed by surgeons. You'll be relieved to know they use modern instruments rather than lumps of rock. It's done in an emergency to relieve a build-up of blood pressure in the brain caused by a blood clot. And, as you now know, people can survive with a hole in the bonce. A person can even survive with a hole made by an accident.

GROANING GAGE

Everyone liked Phineas Gage of Vermont, USA. The young railway foreman was a lively and happy-go-lucky chap. Until one day in 1848...

Phin was blasting a path for a new railway. He was trying to push some dynamite down a hole using an iron bar. When disaster struck...

The dynamite blew up and the iron bar shot straight through Phin's head. The bar was found a few metres away spattered with bits of poor Phin's brains.

Phin was knocked out by the blow but quickly came round and even managed to walk to the doctor's. The hole was big enough for the doctor to put his fingers inside Phin's skull...

Amazingly, Phin lived – although he was ill for a few weeks. But as a result of his injuries he was a changed man. He was moody, foul-mouthed, rude and often drunk.

He lost jobs frequently, but his wits remained sharp. He made money by exhibiting himself in fairs with the iron bar stuck through his head.

Scientists were eager to study Phin's battered bonce. So he sold his body to *several* medical schools for cash up front.

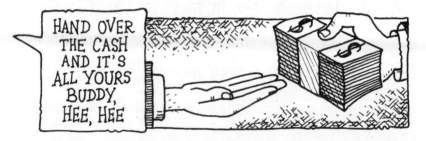

After Phin's death the medical schools argued over who owned the body and, of course, the brain. The doctors were keen to remove Phin's brain and look at the damage.

The doctors found that Phin's brain hadn't been able to repair the damage it suffered. The damaged front cortex area wasn't vital for life but it had clearly shaped Phin's personality.

The famous bar and Phin's skull ended up on display at the museum of Harvard Medical School. I hope they were given a good clean first.

But you don't need a near-fatal brain injury to lose consciousness. No, in fact you do it far less painfully every night when you curl up your tootsies and snuggle down in your nice warm bed. And if that's where you are right now why not take a peek at the next chapter? It's a real dream.

Or is it a nightmare?

NASTY NIGHTMARES

This chapter is about sleep. It's about dreams and it's about nightmares...

Warning to sensitive readers: Are you easily scared and reading this chapter in bed? Well, if you must scream, scream quietly.

But, try not to be too petrified – nightmares and dreams are fascinating effects made by your bulging brain in the middle of sleep. Here are a few more facts to sleep on...

Bulging brains fact file

Name:

Basic facts:

Disgusting details:

BEAT...
BEAT...
...ZZZ

TIRED
TEACHER

Sleep

When you go to sleep you lose consciousness. Your sleeping brain produces delta brainwaves (see page 52) and you're unaware of your surroundings. Oh, so you knew that already? Well, try and stay awake for the next bit.

Staying awake for two weeks can kill you. Scientists believe that the body needs a period of rest each day. Without it, the body gets more and more exhausted and vital functions like heartbeat begin to falter.

So sleep is good for you. And whilst you're lying in bed you can always listen in to those chattering Neuro-phone wires as your brain tries to help you to nod off…

SLEEPY SIGNALS

Cortex to all brain areas: "I'M REALLY WIDE AWAKE. DO I HAVE TO GO TO SLEEP?"

Pineal gland to cortex: "NIGHT-NIGHT, CORTEX. SOME OF THIS NICE MELATONIN WILL CALM YOU DOWN"

SCIENTIFIC NOTE
Melatonin (mel-a tone-in) damps down the activity in the cortex. The pineal gland pumps out melatonin every night on a 24-hour cycle.

Cortex: "YAWN, I'M FEELING REALLY SLEEPY."

RAS* to cortex: "COME ON, CORTEX, TIME YOU WERE TUCKED UP. HERE'S SOME NICE SEROTONIN** TO HELP YOU SLEEP."

SCIENTIFIC NOTE
At this point your brain should lose consciousness.
But you won't notice that bit. Why? Because you'll be asleep, too, stupid.

Cortex: "Zzzz."

* That's the reticular activating system in your brain stem, remember?

** That's the "sensible" chemical that damps down your feelings. The serotonin should calm your cortex down even more.

BULGING BRAIN EXPRESSIONS

Two psychologists are chatting.

Is this dangerous?

ANSWER

No, but it's annoying for everyone else. Somniloquy (som-nil-o-kwee) means talking in your sleep. Somnambulism (som-nam-bew-lis-m) means walking in your sleep. So the psychologist walks and talks in her sleep. Well, could be worse: in 1993 a British businessman had to be rescued by fire-fighters after falling into a rubbish chute. He had fallen in whilst sleepwalking in the nude.

SPOT THE SLEEPWALKER

One in twenty children walk in their sleep and some adults do this when they're feeling stressed. Does your mum/dad/brother/sister/hamster sleepwalk? Here are a few signs to look out for.

A SLEEPWALKING TEACHER

EYES OPEN BUT ASLEEP

BLANK EXPRESSION

mumble, mumble

ER. . . THE LESS SAID ABOUT THIS THE BETTER

TALKING GIBBERISH

Mind you, some teachers act this way on a Monday morning when they are supposedly awake.

A BIT OF AN EYE-OPENER

Any sleep, even with a bit of sleepwalking thrown in, is better than no sleep at all. In the 1960s scientists kept volunteers awake to measure the effects of lack of sleep on their brains and bodies. What you are about to read is a story based on real events that happened in these tests. So try to keep awake for the next few minutes…

HORRIBLE HEALTH WARNING!

Don't try this experiment at home. You might keep parents awake and this can have a magical shrinking effect on pocket money. And, as you are about to find out, losing too much sleep is very unhealthy. For this reason scientists are no longer keen to perform this experiment.

SLEEP DEPRIVATION EXPERIMENT DIARY

by **Arthur Sleep** *(volunteer)*

Notes by **Dr Irma Wake** *(day-shift)* &

Dr Hugh Kant-Dropoff *(night-shift)*

Monday night
I'm wide awake and feel like I could stay awake for ever! I drink coffee to keep me going. The only problem is that Dr Kant-Dropoff insists on coming to the toilet with me to check I don't doze off in there.

4a.m. Tuesday morning. Feeling a bit sleepy: I could do with some shut-eye. I fight the feeling off and play some snooker.

TUESDAY MORNING
Dr Kant-Dropoff writes. . .

Arthur is fine. His heartbeat and reflexes are normal. I wired him up to an EEG machine and his brainwaves are normal. I'm a bit sleepy now myself - could do with a bit of kip. Oh well, off to bed - I'm handing over to Dr Wake who will monitor Arthur during the day.

Tuesday night - I nearly dropped off tonight but Dr Kant-Dropoff rudely shook me and shouted "wakey-wakey" in my ear. I feel really cross with him.

Dr Kant-Dropoff writes. . .

Arthur seems more tired and irritable tonight. Shouted at me at 3 a.m. after I stopped him from falling asleep.

WEDNESDAY
Dr Wake writes. . .

Arthur is slurring his words today. He keeps repeating things and he moves about slowly. He can still play chess, though, and even beat me in a game. Obviously the areas of his brain dealing with thinking are still functioning normally.

Wednesday night - I'm not talking to Dr Kant-Dropoff after last night's row. Played loud music to keep awake. I could see Dr Kant-Dropoff didn't like it - ha-ha!

I'm really tired all the time now. If I close my eyes I could fall asleep. Got to keep going.

Dr Kant-Dropoff writes...

Arthur has been <u>extremely</u> quiet tonight.

Thursday

I don't like the way Dr Wake shouts "rise and shine" each morning. Why does she have to be so cheerful? I mean it's not as if I've been asleep. I bet she gets a good night's sleep, though...she must have something against me. Yes, that's it: she's getting at me.

Dr Wake writes...

Arthur is clearly exhausted and his pulse rate keeps going faster and then slower.

Thursday night - My beans on toast tasted funny tonight: I feel sure Dr Kant-Dropoff put some drug in my food. But why? WHY? Maybe he's getting back at me for playing loud music. I'll show him...

Dr Kant-Dropoff writes...

Arthur seems to be suffering from strange ideas. This is typical of people who lose too much sleep. We'll have to monitor the situation closely.

Friday – Refused to finish my cornflakes this morning – the milk tasted odd. Dr Wake gave them to me so she must be in on the plot with Dr Kant-Dropoff. Ha-ha! They think I don't suspect they tamper with my food.

4.15 p.m. When I stood up the floor was heaving like the sea. I must have been poisoned!

Dr Wake writes...

Arthur appears to be seeing things. I must contact Dr Kant-Dropoff and discuss ending the experiment.

FRIDAY NIGHT
Dr Kant-Dropoff writes...

Arthur has locked himself in the toilet. He keeps shouting for me to keep away and stop poisoning him. I will monitor the situation from the outside. I'm afraid he will use violence.

I'll be safe here. All quiet – I think Dr K-D's gone away. Phew, I can relax! Just close my eyes now for a minute... Zzzzzzzzzz

SATURDAY MORNING
Dr Kant-Dropoff and Dr Wake...

We broke into the toilet and found Arthur fast asleep. He didn't stir when we moved him to a bed.

sunday evening - I've just woken up. I still feel really sleepy but all my tiredness has gone. The last few days seem like a nightmare. Did I really imagine the doctors were trying to poison me? And here they are now, all smiles with some tea and biscuits. They wouldn't harm a fly. That's the last time I miss a night's sleep. ···

CONCLUSION BY Dr Wake and Dr Kant-Dropoff

Arthur seems fully recovered. His pulse, heart-rate and brainwaves are normal. The experiment proves lack of sleep can cause mistaken thoughts and cause other problems such as disorders to the pulse and heartbeat. It appears these can be put right by a longer than usual period of sleep.

BET YOU NEVER KNEW!

Although scientists no longer keep people awake, in one experiment volunteers were woken up as soon as they started to dream. The scientists wanted to find out how the brain would act if it couldn't dream. The poor volunteers ended up getting woken over 30 times a night as their brains tried harder to make them dream. But why is dreaming so important...?

Bulging brains fact file

Name: Dreams

Basic facts: You spend six years of your life dreaming. A dream is made of mixed-up memories which your cortex often makes into a story.

Disgusting details: Scientists think that in the future some kind of camera could be invented to pick up signals in the neurons of your brain and turn them into pictures. So you could watch reruns of your happiest dreams and even your scariest nightmares – if you're brave enough.

Let's imagine it's already possible: this is how it might happen...

The Dream Machine

Congratulations on buying the NEW Dream Machine – the incredible machine that turns dreams into exciting videos.

PLEASE READ THESE INSTRUCTIONS CAREFULLY...

1 To set up the machine, plug it into your TV Strap the brainwave-detecting hat to your head.

2 Go to sleep. Nothing will happen for at least 45 minutes as your body drifts from light to deeper sleep. As you relax your mouth might drop open and start to dribble – this is entirely normal.

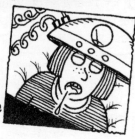

3 After you have been to sleep for about 45 minutes your eyes will start moving under your eyelids. This is also perfectly normal. It is known as rapid eye movement (REM) sleep and it accompanies dreaming.

4 As you dream, your brainwaves will speed up and become irregular. This triggers the dream machine to start recording your dreams.

EEG PRINTOUT

5 You will not be able to move your body whilst dreaming. Your brain squirts a chemical into the brain stem that blocks nerve messages to your muscles. This is a sensible precaution to stop you sleepwalking.

SQUIRT SQUIRT SQUIRT

DON'T MOVE!

BRAIN STEM

6 Relax and enjoy your dream show. Your brain will be going into REM mode about six more times during the night. And the following morning you can replay your video and entertain the whole family with your amazing dreams!

. . . THE KILLER WOODLICE CHASED US TO THE SHORE OF THE CUSTARD SEA. WE JUMPED INTO THE PUDDING BOWLS AND MADE OUR ESCAPE USING GIANT TEASPOONS. CRUMBLE ISLAND CAME INTO SIGHT BUT WE. . .

So what do you think of this invention? It sounds really good, doesn't it? Well, here's something else that will really get your little grey cells buzzing…

EPILOGUE: SOMETHING TO THINK ABOUT

With its billions of neurons and synapses, your bulging brain is the most complicated object in the known universe. So it's no wonder that people find it hard to get their heads round the science of the brain. Even the experts can't make up their minds.

Bishop Nemesius of Emesa (4th century AD) reckoned...

THINKING TAKES PLACE IN THE VENTRICLES

These are the fluid-filled spaces inside the brain, remember. One thousand years later Italian scientist Mondino de Luzzi (14th century) was convinced…

THE LINE OF FLESHY GORE IN THE VENTRICLES IS A WORM THAT CONTROLS THINKING

Yuck! He must have had worms on the brain.

And even modern-day scientists can have misleading ideas on the brain. For example, until the 1980s many scientists believed you could decode what the brain is thinking by looking at the pattern of neuron signals. But it's now known that this pattern varies according to your mood and your level of concentration (see page 146). This means that you can have exactly the same thought and yet each time produce a different pattern of neuron signals.

At present much of what we still don't know about the brain boils down to one awkward little word: why? Why do we have emotions? Why do we sleep?

Or, even over 200 years after Franz Gall started wondering about it...

HMMM!

WHY ARE SUM KIDZ BETTER THAN UTHERS AT SPILLING TESTS?

Question, questions, questions. What do you think?

Thanks to the brilliance of the human brain, people have walked on the moon and explored the depths of the oceans. But at present we still know more about the surface of the moon or the ocean floor than the workings of our own brains. No wonder some people think we'll never find out the whole truth about our brains. They would say…

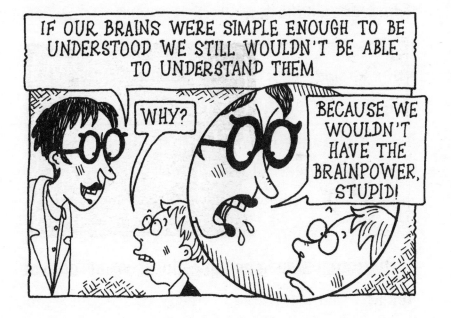

(This does make sense – just you try thinking about it!)

But, on the other hand, it's the mystery that surrounds the brain that makes brain science so exciting. And although bulging brains in tanks or dream machines are still a few years off, scientists regularly make new discoveries. They might find a new brain chemical such as serotonin that affects mood. Or perhaps a new job for an area of the brain. For example, in 2013 US scientists found that zapping part of the limbic system made people more determined to overcome obstacles. Now there's an idea! Maybe brain scientists could motivate their minds by zapping their own brains?

Well, one thing's for sure. Scientists will never cease to search for answers to the questions posed by the brain. And it's the ability to ask questions and to seek out answers that makes us human and our brains so unique.

Now that really is something to think about!

HORRIBLE INDEX